SELLING THE WAR

SELLING THE WAR

Art and Propaganda in World War II

Zbynek Zeman

Exeter Books

NEW YORK

For Lexie

Frontispiece: A line from the
'Star-Spangled Banner' provides
the theme for this 1944 poster for
the US Army Air Forces

Right: A much-needed warning
by G.R. Morris for Britain's
National Safety First Association

Picture Acknowledgments

Acknowledgments and thanks for
permission to reproduce the
posters in this book are due to
Bundesarchiv, Koblenz;
Bibliothèque Nationale, Paris;
Bibliothèque de Nanterre,
Nantes; Imperial War Museum,
London; Library of Congress,
Washington; Musée des Deux
Guerres, Brussels; Musée de la
Guerre, Paris; Musée Royale de
l'Armée, Brussels; New York
Public Library, New York;
Novosti, London; Psywar, St
Albans; Radio Times Hulton
Picture Library, London; Robert
Hunt Library, London; Snark,
Paris; United States National
Archives, Washington; Wiener
Library, London.

© Orbis Publishing Limited, London
1978. First published in USA 1982 by
Exeter Books. Exeter is a trade mark of
Simon & Schuster. Distributed by
Bookthrift, New York, New York.

ISBN 0-89673-124-3
Printed in Hong Kong by
Mandarin Offset International Ltd

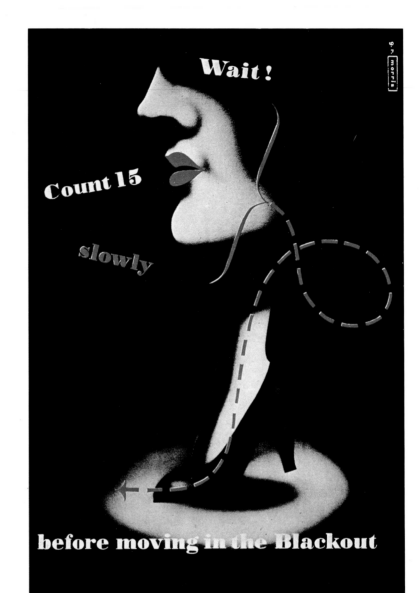

Contents

Introduction 7

Your Country Needs You 31

The Appeal to Patriotism

You Never Know Who's Listening 49

Beating the Spies and Saboteurs

Back Them Up 63

The Campaign for War Production

United We Are Strong 81

The International Crusade

Behold the Enemy 101

The Threat of Barbarism

Bibliography 120

Index 120

Introduction

Posters have become, in this century, one of the many modern instruments of persuasion. They reflect the mood of the time, the styles of their creators, and (in the case of political posters) the preoccupations of politicians and propagandists. They draw on the artistic achievements, in particular the prevalent styles of painting and draughtsmanship, in each country; there is usually a close link between the technical level of commercial advertising and political propaganda. If they are effective, it is because their appeal is direct, immediate, and easily understood.

Because they serve the political purpose of the moment, posters, like most other propaganda materials—pamphlets, broadcasts, banners, leaflets, the mass circulation press, and films—are both ephemeral and disposable. This feature of modern propaganda sets it apart from the artefacts produced by earlier periods, when men had worked with more lasting materials. Those religious movements which allowed themselves to hold images before the believers produced, or patronized the making of, paintings, sculpture or architecture which have survived the centuries. When lay rulers in Europe disputed and inherited one function after another previously discharged by the church, patronage of the visual arts and of architecture was one of them.

Much later, even Adolf Hitler had a longing for permanent memorials. This longing was revealed in his interest in architecture and his grand plans to commemorate his rule; occasionally, he caused pictures—often of himself—to be painted. But at the same time, Hitler operated in an age

Opposite: Citizens of Warsaw study Polish Air Force posters and mobilization notices in August 1939, a few weeks before the German invasion began.

of mass production and was the master of an industrial state. He was one of the originators of modern political pop art. As a young man in Vienna before the First World War, when he was a more or less unemployed tramp who was turned down by the local school of architecture, Hitler sometimes supported himself by painting commercial posters. One of his still-extant posters depicts Vienna's Cathedral of St Stephen, just managing to rise above a mountain of soap bubbles. Young Hitler may not have been aware of the dangers of pollution, but the link between advertising and political propaganda, between the selling of a product and the selling of a politician or political doctrine, was clear to him when he entered politics.

It is no accident that the fascist one-party states of the twentieth century and their leaders gave so much thought to propaganda in all its forms. Mussolini and the Fascists, Hitler and the Nazis, Franco and his Falangists all operated in at least partly industrialized states. They all believed that the individual should be subordinated to the state; they suffered from few inhibitions concerning the desires or views of the individual citizen. In fact, they all embarked on campaigns of national mobilization. So did Lenin and the Bolsheviks, and they, too, concerned themselves with the art of propaganda. But their aims were somewhat different. Lenin wanted to shock the Russian state out of its backwardness; Hitler and Mussolini wanted to make their states bigger, rather than better, or they confused the two goals. However, the problem of how best to mobilize their peoples was common to all of them, and mass propaganda became one of the two main instruments—the other being coercion.

They all used political propaganda consistently and hard in peace-time as well as in war. The western liberal democracies, on the other hand, employed propaganda in war-time only—again, in order to mobilize their peoples and make them more aware of their immediate tasks and goals. Otherwise the liberal democracies dropped propaganda, and most of the institutions which carried it out, as soon as they conveniently could, both after the First and the Second World Wars. There are, of course, election campaigns in these countries, when propaganda temporarily raises its head. There are road safety campaigns or metrication campaigns. Many of the liberal democracies have carried on their Second World War systems of external broadcasts, but this is the only form of propaganda in American, Britain and other West European countries which is carried on on a permanent basis and which is sponsored by the state.

The two wars therefore provided a propaganda explosion when different political systems competed against each other. The competition was for the highest stakes: for the allegiance of their own peoples and the maintenance of their morale; for the demoralization of the enemy and the destruction of his alliances. Nevertheless, the tasks of propaganda in the two world wars were different, and even more so the instruments used. In August 1914 the people, the political parties, the newspapers rallied round their respective governments. There were scenes of wild enthusiasm in the capitals of Europe when the crowds greeted the outbreak of the war. A few months later, this new-found political unity was formalized in the *Burgfrieden* or *union sacré* declarations in the parliaments, establishing a political truce between rival parties for the duration of the war. The task of propaganda was therefore mainly the maintenance of political and social cohesion and of the original enthusiasm for the war.

The outbreak of the Second World War was unaccompanied by such bursts of popular passion. Although it lasted longer than the First World War, it was, in the military and diplomatic senses, a much faster-moving war requiring a greater flexibility and inventiveness on the part of the propagandists. But most important, the first large-scale experiments in the manipulation of public opinion had been made, in the one-party states in particular, before 1939, and new instruments of propaganda were added to those used in the First World War.

Right: First World War Allied propaganda contrasting the high-minded statements of German leaders with the 'facts' of German militarism in action.

8

German Words and German Deeds

"WE see everywhere how our soldiers respect the sacred defence-lessness of woman and child."
Prof. G. Roethe, in "Deutsche Reden in schwerer Zeit."

"AS they continued their advance, the Germans collected about 400 men, women and children (some of the women with babies in their arms) from Campenhout, Elewyt and Malines, and drove them forward as a screen, against the Belgian forces holding the outer ring of the Antwerp lines."
Appendix to the Report of the Bryce Committee.

"WE are still child-like in our inmost feelings, innocent in our pleasures."
Freidrich Lange, in "Reines Deutschtum."

"GONE on the loose and boozed through the streets of Liege."
Diary of a German soldier, quoted in the Bryce Report.

"WE take refuge in our quite peculiar idealism, and dream, alas aloud! of our ideal mission for the saving of mankind."
Hans v. Wolzogen, in "Gedanken zur Kriegszeit."

THE German Secretary of State for the Colonies has admitted that from 1903 to 1913 105,000 natives have been killed in expeditions against them.

"WE thank our German Army that it has kept spotless the shield of humanity and chivalry."
Prof. W. Kahl, in "Deutsche Reden in schwerer Zeit."

"WHILE a number of wounded were being attended to in a Hospital at Gomery, a patrol of the 47th German Infantry appeared and began a general massacre of the wounded and medical staff. The Hospital, full of wounded, was deliberately set on fire."
"Germany's Violation of the Laws of War" (Bland).

"FROM all sides testimonies are flowing in as to the noble manner in which our troops conduct the war."
Pastor J. Rump.

"THE Brigade order is to shoot all Frenchmen who fall into our hands, wounded or not. No prisoners are to be made."
Diary of R. Brenneisen, 112th German Regiment, prisoner in Great Britain.

"IT is true that the breast of every soldier swelled with a noble pride at the thought that he was privileged to wear the German uniform, which history has made a garb of honour above all others."
"Der Deutsche und dieser Krieg," by K. Engelbrecht.

"DETACHED parties were to enter the streets, but actually the Battalion marched in close order into the town, to break into the first houses and loot—no, of course, only to 'requisition'—for wine and other things. Like a wild pack they broke loose, each on their own; officers set a good example by going on ahead. A night in a barracks with many drunk was the end of this day, which aroused in me a contempt I cannot describe."
Extract from the Diary of Gaston Klein.

"THE German soldiers alone are thoroughly disciplined, and have never so much as hurt a hair of a single innocent human being."
H. S. Chamberlain, in "Kriegsaufsatze."

"MY company is at Bouvignes. Our men behave like vandals; everything is upset; the sight of the slaughtered inhabitants defies all description, not a house is left standing. We have dragged out of every corner all survivors, one after another, men, women, and children, found in a burning cloister, and have shot them 'en masse.'"
Diary of a Saxon Officer.

"THE officers of the German Navy, I say it loudly, will always fulfil in the strictest fashion the duties which the unwritten law of humanity and civilization lay on them."
Baron Marschall von Bieberstein, at the Hague Conference.

THE Lusitania was torpedoed without warning on May 7th, 1915, when 1400 men, women, and children were drowned. The Germans struck a special medal to celebrate this event.

"APART from the fighting quality of these troops, their peaceful work behind the fronts bears witness to a thorough spiritual culture."
Houston Stewart Chamberlain, in "Die Zuversicht."

"AT Chauny for two months they (the Germans) had been measuring the cellars of all the houses and calculating the quantity of explosives necessary to blow up each of them; and then after an orgy of pillage, in which they carried off furniture, gutted safes and sacked churches, they systematically destroyed the town in the most thorough and ruthless manner by fires and mines for the space of a fortnight."
Extract from the Proceedings of the French Senate, April 1st, 1917.

"WE Germans represent the latest and the highest achievement of European Kultur."
Prof. A. Lasson, in "Deutsche Reden in schwerer Zeit."

"IN the cemetery of Carlepont, the door of the chapel over the vault of the Swiss family Graffeuried-Villars was carried off. A stone of the vault was prized up, and bones are visible through the aperture. At Candor, two witnesses surprised some Germans in the act of breaking open the tombs of the Trefcon and Censier families. The church to which the cemetery belongs has been shamefully pillaged."
Official Report of the French Commission. Journal Officiel, 18/4/17.

"HOW often in these days has the German soldier been subjected to the temptation to treat the inhabitants of foreign countries with violence and brutality, but everywhere he has obeyed the law, and shown that even in war he knows how to distinguish between the enemy to be crushed and defenceless women and children. The officials and clergy of conquered territory have frequently borne express testimony to this fact."
Pastor M. Hennig, in "Der Krieg und Wir."

"THE names of the priests and of members of the religious orders in the Diocese of Malines who, to my knowledge, have been put to death by the German troops are: Dupierreux, of the Society of Jesus; Sebastian Allard, of the Congregation of Josephites; Brother Candide, of the Congregation of Brothers of Our Lady of Pity; Father Vincent; Professor Carette; Lombaert, Goris, de Clerck, Dergent, Wouters, Van Bladel, Parish Priests. . . ."
Letter of Cardinal Mercier to the German Governor.

"GERMANY is precisely—who would venture to deny it—the representative of the highest morality, of the purest humanity, of the most chastened Christianity."
Pastor H. Francke.

"THE British Steamer, 'Belgian Prince,' was torpedoed by a German submarine on July 31st. The crew abandoned the ship in two boats, and were ordered on to the upper deck of the submarine by the German commander. Under his directions the boats were then smashed with axes and the crew of the 'Belgian Prince' deprived of their lifebelts. The master was taken below and the hatch closed; the submarine submerged without warning with forty-three men standing on her deck. This was the entire crew of the 'Belgian Prince.' With the exception of three all these were drowned."
British Admiralty Report.

J. WEINER LTD. LONDON.

In 1914–18 nobody expected propaganda to win the war. It may not have been conducted in a gentlemanly way by any side, but it was a very minor instrument of war, used in an unhurried way. In London, for instance, an office specializing in propaganda was organized as early as September 1914. Asquith, the Prime Minister, then invited a member of his cabinet, Charles Masterman, Chancellor of the Duchy of Lancaster, to take charge of propaganda. Masterman had been running the national insurance commission at Wellington House, and it was at this address that he set up his inconspicuous propaganda headquarters.

Masterman had been a Cambridge don whose best-known book, *The Condition of England*, was published in 1909. Some of his friends thought that Masterman lacked the common touch in politics; if this was so, he nevertheless was a first-rate publicist. As long as Asquith remained in power and politicians remained either disinterested or suspicious of the value of propaganda, Masterman was undisturbed, turning out his books, leaflets, posters and slogans. But by autumn 1916 a number of government departments had acquired their own information services and then, in November 1916, Asquith, Masterman's friend and protector, left office. The situation remained unsettled until early in 1918, when Lord Beaverbrook was put in charge of the new Ministry of Information. By that time, Masterman's originally modest enterprise had developed into a minor state industry. Lloyd George referred to 'our propaganda, costing I dare not tell the government how much . . .'. In fact, Beaverbrook was able to cut the proposed budget of his ministry from £1,800,000 to £1,200,000. It supported the smallest government department.

The organizational structure of propaganda was developed slowly and so were the vehicles for the delivery of its message. They were always primitive, sometimes crude; most of them—with the exception perhaps of some of the First World War posters—would have been unusable in the second war. For instance, the Bryce report on the conduct of the Germans in Belgium was the best-known of Masterman's publications. It was printed in some thirty languages, appearing on 14 May 1915, a week after the sinking of the *Lusitania*. No book played such a prominent role in the Second World War, though similar messages of the horribleness of the enemy were put across. But this was done in a simpler and briefer manner.

In addition, the original angle of Masterman's propaganda was rather selective. It was mainly aimed at the Americans; Masterman was responsible for coining the slogan 'Hands Across the Sea'. He and his assistants quickly learned to package the bestiality of the enemy under such labels as 'Lusitania' or 'Belgium' or 'Edith Cavell', the nurse who was executed by the Germans for helping Allied soldiers to escape. But the message was put across by the printed word or picture alone, in posters, pamphlets, leaflets, books, and newspapers.

Apart from attempts at the manipulation of public opinion at home, therefore, America became the main propaganda battle-ground. In this way, the antagonists learned their early lessons in psychological warfare and the political and social facts to which it had to relate. British propaganda to the United States was more effective than German, with one exception: after the Easter Rising in Dublin in 1916, the sudden, stark announcement of the executions of the revolutionaries outraged Irish-Americans. Nevertheless, the Germans kept on making blunders all the time. The British had much going in their favour in the United States: not only the common language, but also similar attitudes. More Americans knew their Shakespeare than their Goethe: they believed, say, that the Duke of Wellington rather than Blucher won the battle of Waterloo.

Masterman pioneered the technique of creation by propaganda of popular, simple images. The Germans had a lot to learn from the direct, crisp appeal of British war-time propaganda; they were to learn the lesson well, perhaps ultimately to their disadvantage. At home, Masterman's

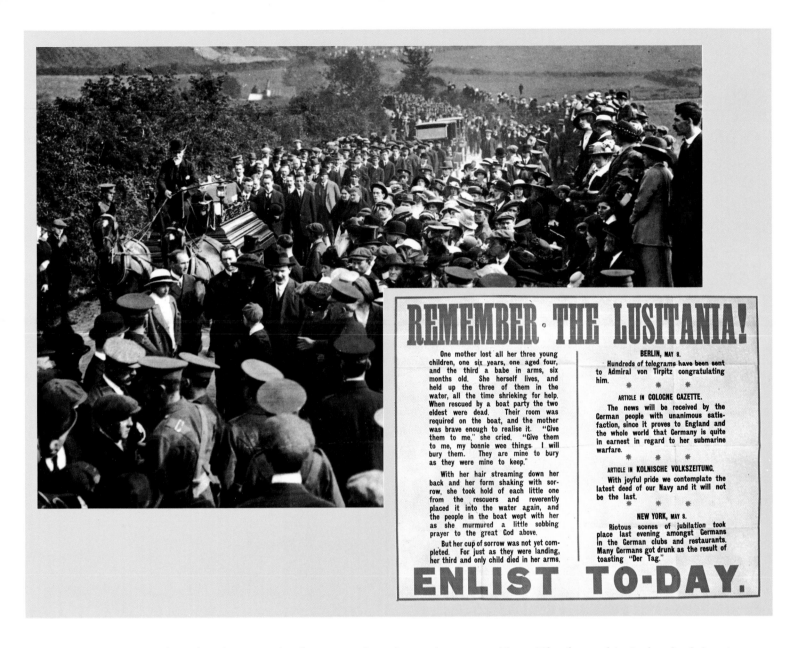

REMEMBER • THE LUSITANIA!

One mother lost all her three young children, one six years, one aged four, and the third a babe in arms, six months old. She herself lives, and held up the three of them in the water, all the time shrieking for help. When rescued by a boat party the two eldest were dead. Their room was required on the boat, and the mother was brave enough to realise it. "Give them to me," she cried. "Give them to me, my bonnie wee things. I will bury them. They are mine to bury as they were mine to keep."

With her hair streaming down her back and her form shaking with sorrow, she took hold of each little one from the rescuers and reverently placed it into the water again, and the people in the boat wept with her as she murmured a little sobbing prayer to the great God above.

But her cup of sorrow was not yet completed. For just as they were landing, her third and only child died in her arms.

BERLIN, MAY 8.
Hundreds of telegrams have been sent to Admiral von Tirpitz congratulating him.

*   *   *

ARTICLE IN COLOGNE GAZETTE.
The news will be received by the German people with unanimous satisfaction, since it proves to England and the whole world that Germany is quite in earnest in regard to her submarine warfare.

*   *   *

ARTICLE IN KOLNISCHE VOLKSZEITUNG.
With joyful pride we contemplate the latest deed of our Navy and it will not be the last.

*   *   *

NEW YORK, MAY 8.
Riotous scenes of jubilation took place last evening amongst Germans in the German clubs and restaurants. Many Germans got drunk as the result of toasting "Der Tag."

ENLIST TO-DAY.

work was later carried on by the press lords: Beaverbrook, Rothermere and Northcliffe. They commanded a formidable pool of talent, and their knowledge of the audience they had courted for many years before the war was unrivalled. They created the kind of publicity which helped the soldiers and civilians over the last months of the war, and which helped to destroy the morale of the enemy.

The simple slogans of Masterman and his successors translated easily into visual terms; indeed, First World War posters were some of the most effective of all the propaganda materials churned out by the war. An appeal to the women of Britain; Lord Kitchener and 'Your Country Needs You!': those posters captured the mood of the time and appealed strongly to the fund of patriotism without which the war could not be carried on.

Nevertheless, the modern forms of propaganda—leaflets dropped from aircraft, broadcasting (the most powerful propaganda weapon of the Second World War) and films—were not yet in existence, or were not used, in the first war. There was, however, one stroke of genius which deserves a mention here, a naval action which pointed to the shape of things to come. The British realized the key importance of communications for the conduct of the war. The first British naval action therefore took place a few hours after midnight on 4 August 1914: *HMS Telsonia* ripped up the cables between Hamburg and New York, off the North Sea coast where the German and Dutch borders met. After that the Germans had to use either

Top: The funeral in Ireland of the victims of the Lusitania *sinking. This event became the focus of much First World War Allied propaganda, especially material aimed at the United States. Above is a poster which appeared in the following week.*

a roundabout cable route or wireless messages anybody could pick up. In terms of communications, and therefore of propaganda strategy, the British had won the first and essential round.

In the view of the Germans, they also won the last round. In fact, the theory of the effectiveness of Allied propaganda in the closing stages of the First World War became a part of the Nazi myth. The 'stab-in-the-back' thesis—that the German army remained undefeated, while the civilian hinterland, under the influence of Allied propaganda, became revolutionized and incapable of carrying on the war and supporting the army—was given much publicity by the extreme German nationalists after 1918. Hitler's opinion, for instance, of the effectiveness of German propaganda in the First World War was very low; it was very flattering on the effectiveness of Allied propaganda.

In the original meaning of the word, propaganda had been a vehicle for a religious faith. This was the way in which Pope Gregory XV used the words when he founded the *Congregatio de Propaganda Fide* in 1662. It was a defensive action to preserve the true Catholic faith, and an organization was created to carry it out. Later, the Marxist and Social Democratic parties on the Continent used the term in a similar way. They had in their possession a doctrine, a 'great fortune' as many of them saw it; propaganda was a vehicle for the doctrine, a way of giving it a much wider currency. The Russian Bolsheviks, however, made a sharp distinction between propaganda and agitation. The latter was a way of influencing the masses, a routine, day-to-day task of creating the mood suited to the political necessity of the day—almost a matter of advertising, in Western terms.

There are memorable examples of early Soviet achievements in the field of agitation. The arrival, for instance, of Lenin at the Finland station one day in April 1917: the crowds, the flowers in Lenin's hand, the military searchlights carving sharp, momentary patterns in the night sky—this passing moment was commemorated in many paintings, its geometry imitated in many variations ever since. And the early Soviet posters, putting machinery, electricity, and the party in the place of the older trinity; making new and simple points for the benefit of war-weary and sometimes ignorant masses. Propaganda, on the other hand, was used to teach the Soviet party *élite* Marxist-Leninist doctrine—a different matter from agitation. Nevertheless, the *agitprop* department in the central committee married the two functions; it is, nowadays, one of the key organizations in the Soviet, and in all the other East European, socialist states.

As it happened, there was no need for Hitler to make any distinction between propaganda and agitation. He had no consistent doctrine to pass on to his followers, apart from his dreadful racialist theory. The few ideas which occurred to the Nazis, or which they tried to assimilate, came and went; the scholars who have tried, since the war, to examine the sources of Nazi ideology have found some difficulties in agreeing on what it actually was. Hitler pursued naked political power, and for that pursuit, propaganda became his favoured means. Propaganda and organization: in Hitler's view, closely connected, constantly interacting, and supremely important. In *Mein Kampf*, the book Hitler wrote in the Landsberg prison after the failed Munich *putsch* of 1923, Hitler put the matter simply: 'The task of propaganda is to attract followers; the task of organization to win members. A follower of a movement is one who declares himself in agreement with its aims; a member is one who fights for it.' He also knew that his propaganda acted as an agent of natural selection: 'The more radical and inciting my propaganda was, the more it frightened off weaklings and irresolute characters and prevented their pushing into the first nucleus of the organization.'

Here, Hitler had a very specific point in mind. It was the calculated connection between propaganda and violence; a small and unenviable inheritance the Nazi movement has left to posterity. The 'beer cellar brawls' were a constant feature of the early history of the party in Munich; later, before 1933, the Nazis succeeded in turning the streets of German towns into battlefields.

In an official text book for German youth which was published in Berlin shortly before the Second World War [Philipp Buehler, *Kampf um Deutschland*, 1938, pp. 46–7] the author flatly stated that, in the early 1920s, 'The greatest difficulty of the party was that nobody took any notice of it.' But brawls at meetings helped; 'Now at last,' he went on in a bright, didactic manner, which was thought to be suitable for the young, 'the party had found the means of shaking the newspapers from their icy reserve! Here was the rope by which it could pull itself up from the depths of being ignored into the daylight of "public opinion". . . . From now on, every opportunity was grasped to answer even the most insignificant provocation by a real chucking out [of their enemies from Nazi meetings]. And lo and behold! From this time on, the bourgeois and the Red press dealt with the naughty Nazis almost every day.'

Here we have the first practical contribution of Hitler and the Nazis to the art of propaganda, which, after 1939, became absorbed into the larger, institutionalized violence of the war. But there were other contributions. For some fifteen years, in and out of power, in peace and in war, the Nazis practised that art. They did so in an industrial state; they believed their own propaganda; their view of its effectiveness was high. Ultimately, they gave propaganda such a bad name that Pope Gregory XV would probably have been profoundly shocked by their usages.

The Nazi theory of propaganda was written into the key parts of *Mein Kampf*. There, in the two relevant chapters, Hitler summarized his views on the subject. His views affected the subsequent course of history—the fortunes of Hitler and his party especially. Indeed, for Hitler, almost every aspect of political activity was synonymous with propaganda; it was a way of pulling himself up by his bootstraps into prominence.

Hitler saw the First World War as the proper beginning of the practice of propaganda; we have noted the low view he had of Germany's effort in that respect. But young Hitler had had an opportunity of observing earlier propaganda in action in Vienna before 1913. He acknowledged his debt to, as he put it, the 'Marxist Socialists': they had mastered the instrument which was, at that time, disregarded by the middle-class parties.

Throughout his consideration of the subject it is apparent that Hitler was not much concerned with the actual content of propaganda. The fascination propaganda had for him was largely of a technical nature. It was a problem of salesmanship on a mass market; of the opportunities presented by the entry of half-educated masses into that market. He straightaway formed a low opinion of his potential audience. He thought that the masses were malleable, corrupt, or corruptible; their sentiment being 'not complex, but simple and consistent'. The proper task of propaganda was, for Hitler, to bring a few subjects within the field of vision of the masses; for his purposes, the intellectuals were of no importance. Propaganda therefore had to concentrate on a few points; it had to hammer them in constantly; its appeal had to be emotional, not rational. It had to present its subjects in black-and-white terms; it could not afford to make any concessions to the adversary. In Hitler's propaganda, there was to be no place for the qualifying clause.

Nor did it matter to Hitler whether the contents of his propaganda bore any resemblance to reality. Hitler was quite explicit on this point. Poison gas had to be fought by poison gas, as Hitler saw it; lies had to be countered with still bigger lies; and if these failed, there were violence, horror and intimidation to fall back on.

Propaganda was therefore, together with the party organization, Hitler's most important asset when he embarked on his political career after the First World War. And the right blend of the various components of propaganda was of vital importance. First, there was Hitler's public speaking. He was convinced that all the important revolutionary events of the past had been caused by the spoken, not the written, word. He had in mind especially the relationship between the speaker and the audience. Hitler was at his most effective when his message began reaching his audience through a haze of mass hysteria; he preferred to convince individuals through the masses, rather than the other way round. That point was again made when, after 1933, Goebbels, his propaganda minister, tried to put Hitler into a recording studio to deliver a speech. The immediate rapport between Hitler and his audience was interrupted; the speech fell flat, and Goebbels never repeated the experiment in peacetime.

Hitler wanted to be, as a young man, an artist or an architect; he was intensely conscious of the visual appeal his movement presented to the outside world. He knew the importance for men of belonging to a group, and the importance for the group to have easily recognizable visual symbols. He designed the standard of the *Sturmabteilung* (SA)—the para-military arm of the Nazi movement—himself, giving careful attention to every detail. There was the eagle at the top; Hitler was apparently attracted to the bird because he had found it described, in an anti-Semitic encyclopedia, as the 'Aryan [*i.e.* non-Jew] in the world of animals.' Underneath, there was the swastika—the *Hakenkreuz*, the key emblem of the movement, of ancient origin and representing the sun—surrounded

Below: Storm-troopers at Nuremberg in 1935, surrounded by posters advertising the anti-Semitic periodical Der Stürmer.

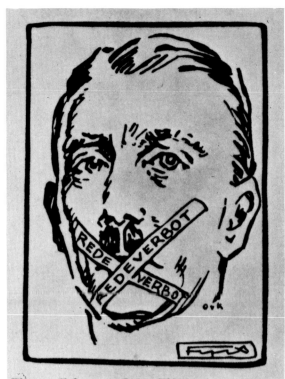

Einer allein von 2000 Millionen Menschen der Erde darf in Deutschland nicht reden!

Top: An early Nazi poster protesting against the ban on Hitler's speeches in 1926. Above: A poster urging Germans to throw off their ties to the Jews and vote for Nazis.

by a wreath of laurel leaves. There were the Nazi songs, the *Heil* greeting, the party rallies, all the paraphernalia of a small, hard-working party on the make. This was at a time when the liberal democracies had dismantled their wartime propaganda machinery; when Lenin and the Bolsheviks, and later Stalin, built up and made use of their *agitprop* department to transform the Soviet Union into an industrial state, and to consolidate the position of their party in that state; and after Mussolini, who probably gave less attention to propaganda than Hitler did, and more to his own image and oratory, had come into power in Italy.

But it should be stressed that, in the 1920s, German and other European propagandists were still travelling light in terms of the technical equipment at their disposal. Broadcasting and films were still being developed, and in any case, Hitler did not have much access to them before 1933. At the early meetings of the party he had to rely on the carrying power of his voice alone; only in 1930 did microphones and loudspeakers become standard equipment at Nazi meetings.

In the absence of other media, posters—in Germany and elsewhere—played the key role in political campaigning. There are the early anti-Semitic posters: the 'string-puller', the towering Jew with strings reaching out from his pockets to the small, shadowy figures of the massed workers surrounding him; there is the 1926 poster, when Hitler was banned from speaking publicly in several of the German states, with the caption 'he alone of the 2,000 million people on the earth is not allowed to speak in Germany', with sticking plaster across Hitler's mouth and moustache.

There is one photograph which conveys the mood of the Nazi movement before the war better than any other. It was taken after the party rally in Nuremberg in 1935. Three identical storm-troopers, with their backs to the photographer, their backsides not quite fitting into their ill-tailored breeches, walk to a tram stop past a wall with three identical anti-Semitic posters. That arid photograph shows how the Germans, much more than any other Europeans at the time, spent their lives surrounded by posters and by their own inane propaganda.

By 1926, Hitler had acquired the services of Dr Joseph Goebbels, and sent him to run the crucial party organization in Berlin. Goebbels, who had written a novel as a young man, was an exception among Nazi leaders. He was an intellectual who happened to be crippled; cool, detached, yet totally dedicated to Hitler. As a speaker, he was an accomplished performer: his effects precisely calculated, he switched emotion on and off. He could stand back, look at his performance, and enquire about its impact. The only time when he came near to believing his propaganda was when he was engaged in carefully constructing the propaganda image of Adolf Hitler. He had a feudal loyalty to the leader.

At first, Hitler was presented to the Germans as a spokesman of a hard-pressed generation which had fought and lost a just war. The belted mackintosh, the hat with its brim turned down, the beer-cellar fights and the street-fights, added up to the image of an ex-serviceman in a civilian uniform who carried on the fight. Then Goebbels brought out Hitler's qualities: will-power and ability, with luck thrown in for good measure. Then there was Hitler the prophet, who had experienced the Germans' 'racial misery'; Hitler the fighter; Hitler the understanding human being.

After 1933, when the Nazis grasped supreme power in Germany, Goebbels released the full charisma of the leader. He had taken up the work of Bismarck and was about to complete it. He was 'revered by the overwhelming majority of the people.' Hitler's charisma, however, had to be respectable: Goebbels's work on his behalf before the war culminated in a sombre poster, a half-length picture of Hitler, heavily touched up, with the hard-hitting caption: '*Ein Volk, ein Reich, ein Führer*' ('One nation, one empire, one leader'). In 1939 it replaced religious pictures and crucifixes on the walls of thousands of offices and classrooms.

Left: Goebbels encourages the German people to greater sacrifices as the war turns against the Axis. Below: A Russian caricature of the Minister for Propaganda at work in 1943.

Ein Volk, ein Reich, ein Führer

Left: One of the most popular posters of the Führer, designed under Goebbels's directions early in 1939. Above: 'All Germany hears the Führer'—and anything else the Minister of Propaganda decided it should hear.

Hitler wanted to unite all the Germans living in Europe; he wanted to reopen for them the East of the continent where the Slavs, who were in his view vastly racially inferior to the Germans, could easily be subjected to Nazi conquest. There was the *Anschluss* of Austria in 1938; the destruction of Czechoslovakia in 1938 and 1939; and finally, the war with Poland, on 1 September 1939, which both Britain and France joined two days later.

The political crisis occasioned by Hitler led to the reconstitution in the West of the instruments of propaganda. The British set up, before the outbreak of the war, the Department of Propaganda to the Enemy and Enemy-Controlled Territories, which later became converted into the Department for Enemy Propaganda; the Ministry of Information also reappeared. The Department for Enemy Propaganda recruited a large staff, including many refugees from continental countries; it took some time before it was forged into an effective propaganda weapon. There were two other organizations in London concerning themselves with propaganda: the Political Intelligence Department in the Foreign Office and the BBC. In order to coordinate the activities of the three organizations which were concerned with foreign propaganda, the Political Warfare Executive was set up in 1939; its task was to direct, organize and supervise psychological warfare against the enemy. Sir Robert Bruce Lockhart, who had spent much of his time before the war as a diplomat in East Europe, became the PWE head.

After Hitler's attack on the USSR on 22 June 1941, there was no need for the Soviets to make new organizational arrangements for the conduct of their propaganda. As before, the *agitprop* department of the central committee was responsible for propaganda at home: it kept in touch with the 7th Department of Political Administration of the Red Army in Moscow, which was responsible, together with the lower-level political organs of the army, for the conduct of propaganda to the enemy.

The political detachments of the Red Army were equipped with stationary and mobile printing presses; they concentrated on leaflet propaganda aimed at the enemy and his morale. With the establishment of the front-line organization 'Free Germany', Soviet propaganda to the enemy moved into a higher gear. For instance the picture postcard entitled *Heil Beil!*, which depicted Hitler's face as an axe, was effective and, in a gruesome way, funny: this was 'black propaganda', since the provenance of the postcard purported to have been *OKW Offsetdruck*, Leipzig.

In general, Red Army propaganda pursued the following aims:

to prove the unjust nature of the war started by German fascist imperialism;

to demonstrate the imperialist character of German fascism and its ideology and the way it was an enemy of people;

to show the activities of the Nazi party in practice, and the way they drove the German people into the war;

to discredit the German leaders and show the contradictions between them and the German people;

to demonstrate the growth of the anti-fascist movement in the countries under German occupation;

to develop and stimulate the conviction in the inevitable breakdown of fascism and of the fascist state.

Front-line propaganda, especially in the last two years of the war, was complemented by the 're-education' of German PoWs in the USSR.

Despite the propaganda by the Western Allies in favour of the Soviet Union after Hitler's attack in June 1941, there was in practice no cooperation between the Western allies and the Soviets with regard to propaganda. The geographical and ideological distances were too large. On the other hand, Anglo-American cooperation, after America's entry into the war in December 1941, was very close. The US Office for War Information was established in June 1942 and opened a branch in London; it kept in close touch with the PWE throughout the war. The two offices issued, for instance, some joint leaflets; the first major Anglo-American propaganda campaign accompanied the TORCH operation, when the Americans landed in North Africa in November 1942. Later, mainly based on experiences gained during the North African campaign, the Psychological Warfare Division was established at the Supreme Headquarters of the Allied Expeditionary Forces in Europe (PWD/SHAEF) under General McLure. Nevertheless, the two top civilian organizations, the PWE and the OWI, carried on their activities independently from the military.

With the exception of the Soviet Union—though even the Russians had to improvise a lot at the front line, especially in the early stages of the war—the Allied war propaganda effort was organized on an *ad hoc* basis; Goebbels, on the other hand, had all the propaganda instruments at hand when the war broke out. But this put neither the Germans nor Goebbels into a position of clear advantage.

On the credit side, Goebbels had succeeded, in the six years of peace Hitler had allowed the Germans after the establishment of the Nazi state,

Above: 'Hail the Hatchet!'—a Soviet attack on Nazi barbarism on the Eastern front after the invasion in June 1941.

Above left and above: A Russian satire on Hitler's ill-fated march to Moscow; the Blitzkrieg drum has finally burst.

in consolidating the position of his ministry of propaganda, or *Promi* for short. There had been the inevitable clash between *Promi* and the foreign ministry as to who was responsible for the conduct of foreign propaganda. The development of that conflict was reflected in the allocation of funds to the two ministries before the war. In 1934, 21.6m DM were spent on *Promi* and 42.8m DM on the foreign ministry. In 1935, the difference narrowed: 40.82 and 46.8m DM were spent respectively on the two ministries. In 1937, *Promi* shot ahead with an expenditure of 55.3m, compared with 49.4m spent on the foreign ministry. But then, in December 1937, a new Nazi, Ribbentrop, replaced a diplomat of the old school, von Neurath, in the foreign ministry, and the balance of expenditure on the two ministries started being restored. Nevertheless, expenditure on diplomacy did not catch up with the funds lavished on propaganda in the last two years before the war.

Apart from the favoured position of *Promi* in the hierarchy of government departments, Goebbels enjoyed another advantage. He had learned to use broadcasting abroad in the course of many pre-war crises. Before the Saarland referendum in May 1934, Goebbels carried out a programme of saturation broadcasting to the province, and about the province to the Germans; then there were the Ruhr, the Austrian and the Czechoslovak crises. The Nazi broadcasters learned the trick of creating a 'bridge' between the Germans and their compatriots abroad; of producing a feeling of community between them so strong that it amounted to the reality of national unity. They learned to disregard political divisions between the Germans and to create the impression of German nationalism as a spontaneous force which knew no obstacles. This was the strength and the

Gorilla „ADOLF"
Vorsicht!
Tottmilig!

DA GEHÖRT ER HIN
DA KOMMT ER HIN!

*Above: 'Gorilla Adolph' behind bars—
'That's where he belongs, and that's where
he's going'. This Soviet propaganda
postcard was distributed on the Eastern
front by the Red Army's political units.*

weakness of Nazi propaganda: it was calculated to appeal to the Germans alone, and more and more often it did. But its appeal elsewhere fell flat. Before, during and after the Munich crisis, for instance, the Germans did not bother to broadcast to the Czechs in their own language.

Apart from its intense all-German provincialism there were other weaknesses in Germany's propaganda. First, the manipulators of public opinion were themselves used to being manipulated. In all the departments of *Promi* a stream of directives constantly percolated from one level to another: initiative, inventiveness, independence became submerged in the quicksands of totalitarian bureaucracy. Secondly, from the top to the bottom of that bureaucracy, there existed a kind of organizational anarchy. Hitler himself did not bother much about these administrative overlaps which led to hostility between departments and their heads. He probably preferred it that way, at any rate at the top of the Nazi heap; it made everyone less certain of himself and more dependent on Hitler. Finally, there was Goebbels's own position. Shortly before the war, Goebbels wanted to divorce his wife and marry a Czech (*i.e.* racially inferior, in Nazi terms) actress; Hitler intervened, the girl was booted out of Berlin, and Goebbels returned to his wife and children. In a way, the war years were for Goebbels a long climb back into Hitler's favour.

But Goebbels and propaganda were in some difficulties in any case. The point about Hitler was that he always eagerly grasped every new instrument of power. Propaganda had helped him and his party into political prominence; after 1933, Hitler had at his disposal the whole machinery of the state. There were too many interests competing for his attention and favour, and as the war drew nearer the army became Hitler's abiding interest. A week after the invasion of Poland, on 8 September 1939, Hitler issued a command concerning propaganda. It stated that *Promi* remained the 'central agency for the practical application of propaganda. Breaking it up during the war would be comparable to breaking up certain components of the *Wehrmacht*.' Only 'certain components': the big battalions were on the march, and Goebbels had to find out how he could best assist them. He was right when he said that Hitler would 'soon listen to his generals only, and it will be very difficult for me.'

The *ad hoc*, improvising organization of their propaganda did not work to the disadvantage of the Western Allies. The new British propagandists were dons and writers, journalists and lawyers; they came to their task with fresh, open minds; there was some eccentricity, and a lot of independence of mind, in their ranks. They knew their domestic audience well. When they were not well acquainted with their foreign audiences, the British did not hesitate to ask refugees from continental Europe to assist them with their propaganda abroad. Unlike the Germans, the British had no inhibitions in drawing on expert knowledge.

Nor were the organizational and administrative kinks as apparent in London as they were in Berlin. Of the four bodies engaged in propaganda —the Ministry of Information, the Political Warfare Executive, the Political Intelligence Department and the BBC—only the BBC was a permanent institution. With regard to external propaganda, the PWE formulated policy; the PID gathered intelligence from as many sources as it could; the BBC implemented the policy through broadcasting.

Early in 1938, the BBC had started broadcasts to the Middle East in Arabic, mainly to counter Italian attacks in the same medium on Britain. A few months later, in September, the corporation decided to run services to Europe, in French, German and Italian in the first place; after the outbreak of the war, services to the occupied countries were added.

For domestic and external propaganda throughout the war, broadcasting was doubtless the leading medium on both sides. It left all the other forms of propaganda—newspapers, leaflets, posters, even films—far behind. It was easier to control and direct centrally than the newspapers; it needed much less manpower; above all, it was immediate, up-to-the-minute, and its message usually penetrated. Goebbels said, before the war, 'What the press was for the nineteenth century, wireless will be for the twentieth. One could change Napoleon's words, and call it the Eighth Great Power.' For Goebbels, broadcasting remained the preferred medium. But broadcasting punctured the international law concerning the 'sovereignty of air space', and with that it ruled out, to the Nazi's growing discomfort, the monopoly of information.

Despite the privileged position of broadcasting, war-time propaganda developed a great multiplicity of forms, including *Flüsterpropaganda*— 'whispered propaganda'—an underground, alternative form. But in Germany some whispered propaganda was initiated by *Promi* and other official agencies; this made it technically 'black' whispered propaganda, perhaps the most abstruse of the propaganda art forms.

'Black'—'grey'—'white': propaganda was classified according to its origin. White propaganda gave its source openly: the BBC news, or an OKW communique. Grey propaganda left the audience to guess, not indicating its source. Black propaganda pretended to be what it was not: for instance a leaflet, addressed to the enemy, and claiming to come off his own printing presses. In Germany in the later stages of the war, whispered propaganda was supposed to be reliable because it was unmanipulated and of spontaneous, popular origin. A piece of official information inserted into the network therefore at once became black propaganda.

In the first phase of the war, Hitler and his armies could do nothing wrong. This run of good luck included the *Blitzkrieg* campaigns in Poland, in Scandinavia, in the Low Countries, in France. The triumphant OKW (*Oberkommando der Wehrmacht*, or Army High Command) bulletins, preceded and terminated by a triumphant fanfare, were heard everywhere on the wireless and the communications system—in the streets, in factories, in Germany and in more and more towns of occupied Europe. Here, for propaganda purposes, Goebbels employed the same techniques as he had done in Germany. Under the guidance of *Promi*, uniformity was swiftly imposed on the means of mass communication. New newspapers, or old newspapers under new editorial managements, began to appear; new controllers were installed at the broadcasting stations; the countries of occupied Europe became a monopoly market for Goebbels's films, travelling exhibitions, posters, and other artefacts of propaganda.

Until the invasion of the Soviet Union, German propaganda concerning the new-found unity of anti-Bolshevik Europe was uncertain in its conception and execution. Hostility to Britain and her exclusion from the continent were the only constant themes. Defeated France proved difficult to integrate into Goebbels's schemes; the *Grossraum* ('big space') projects concerning the Mediterranean and North Africa became bogged down by military and political uncertainty, and especially by the need to reserve a special place in South Europe for Germany's ally, Mussolini.

Although some striking technical successes were scored in the uniformity of the means of information in occupied Europe, the construction of the concept *Festung Europa*—Fortress Europe—was incomplete until the attack on the Soviet Union. After the summer of 1941, German publicity on this key item came into a sharper focus. Hitler himself explained his attack on Russia by a British–Bolshevik conspiracy; Hitler's favoured propaganda themes started then fitting better together. The anti-British, the anti-Bolshevik and the anti-Semitic and racial themes could be underscored by the conspiracy theories, to which the Nazis had always been very partial.

Towards the end of June 1941, the German press was instructed that 'reports from the whole world make it apparent that a rising of all Europe against Bolshevism can be noted. . . . Europe marches against the

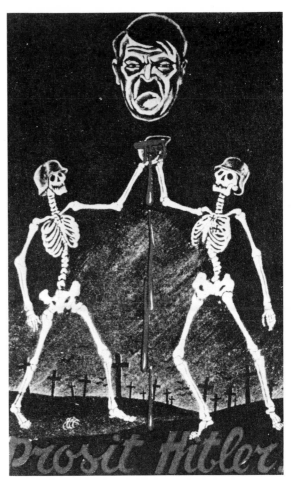

Above: A toast in blood to Hitler. Like the 'Gorilla Adolph' postcard, this was Soviet 'black' propaganda; it purported to come from the Germans' own presses.

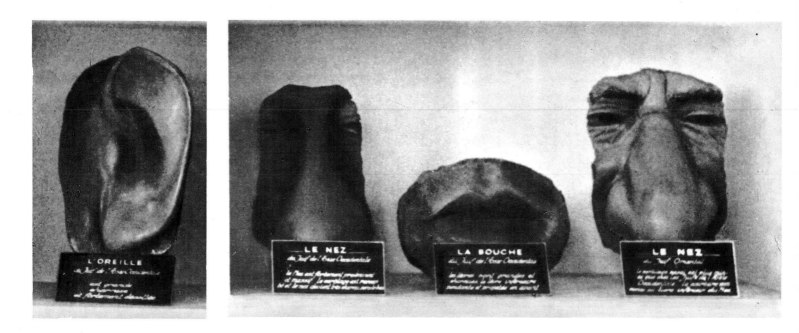

Above: 'Typical Jewish features' as seen in occupied France. 'Every Frenchman', the spectators were told, 'who is determined to combat the Hebrew menace must learn how to recognize the Jew'. Opposite: A poster advertising a similar exhibition in Paris. Such displays came under the authority of Goebbels's propaganda ministry.

common enemy in unique solidarity. . . . This hour of birth of the new Europe is being accomplished without any pressure from the German side. . . . Newspapers are faced here with the immense task, as it is essential, especially with regard to America, that the unity of Europe in the fight against Bolshevism is made clear to the new world as well. . . .' The campaign in the East added a new dimension to the Nazi European publicity. There were two civilizations in Europe, the Nazis insisted, and theirs was vastly superior. The *Judeo-Bolshewismus* had to be defeated if European civilization was to survive; otherwise it would be submerged by the robot-like, sub-human creatures from the East, the *Untermenschen* of Nazi propaganda; in the words of Goebbels, by the 'blunted human material of the East without a will of its own.'

Less than a year after the invasion of the USSR, in the spring of 1942, the early boasting, bombastic note disappeared from Goebbels's propaganda; the Minister of Propaganda evolved a new, more realistic, sombre line. Though the second offensive on the Eastern front was going well, there was no question of a *Blitzkrieg* victory. Again, as in the First World War, the centre of Europe was faced with an alliance between the East and the West. The war, Goebbels was convinced, had become harder. Then there was the North African battle of Alamein in October 1942; in February 1943 the German Sixth Army surrendered at Stalingrad; and all the time, the intensity of Allied air-raids on Germany was growing. Very visibly, the fortunes of the war were no longer going one way only. Hitler had been losing his touch as a speaker for some time; Goebbels noted this and did his best to fill the gap. From the end of 1942 he began to conduct a propaganda of pessimism. It was modelled on Churchill's example, but this was not quite what the Germans expected of their formerly victorious, charismatic leaders.

Early in 1943, therefore, Goebbels again and again made the point that the Germans would have to conduct a *total* war. 'The enemy wants to destroy us totally: let us therefore wage war totally, in order to bring about a total victory.' And he told the departmental heads of his ministry on 4 January 1943 that 'I myself want to disappear from my mind and from the mind of the ministry the idea that we cannot lose the war. Of course we can lose the war. The war can be lost by people who will not exert themselves; it will be won by those who try the hardest. We must not believe fatalistically in certain victory: we must have a positive view.' And finally, Goebbels made the 'total war' speech at the *Sportpalast* in Berlin on 18 February 1943, a dramatic high-water mark of his career. Nevertheless, propaganda, Goebbels may well have reflected, could not

MICHEL
JACQUOT
SEPTEMBRE - OCTOBRE
EXPOSITION
LE JUIF
ET LA FRANCE
PALAIS BERLITZ . 31 Bd DES ITALIENS

The Po is waiting for you

PADOVA

VERONA

MANTOVA

ROVIGO

FERRARA

MODENA

دریائے پو تمہارا انتظار کر رہا ہے

Above and opposite: The two sides of a leaflet aimed at Allied troops in Italy. Following the Allied invasions, the Germans made effective use of parodies of tourist brochures.

Opposite below: This German leaflet pointed out to the British and American troops in Italy that their advance had been considerably slower than a snail's.

take the place of military success. Some Nazi leaders probably thought it could. A memorandum was in circulation on the highest party levels in 1943, probably drafted by Martin Bormann, which argued that propaganda should return under the full control of the party. Propaganda should again become what it used to be in the heroic age of the party before 1933: an instrument for the achievement of instant success.

From 1943, the Allies started winning propaganda battles as well as military ones. In 1940 and 1941 the BBC had seriously misreported, on its European service, the effects of RAF raids on German towns. Severe damage was claimed on several occasions when the bombs were in fact dropped far away from the targets. Nevertheless, these were isolated instances; the main tenor of British propaganda was epitomized in the speeches by Churchill: hard-bitten and cautious, gloomy but determined and unyielding. It took Goebbels almost three years before he learned the trick.

Elsewhere in the hierarchy the London-based propagandists were permitted some licence. When, in January 1942, the Japanese were making rapid advances in the war in the Far East, a commentator on the BBC German service said: 'Many of us in Great Britain are not satisfied about the way in which our strategy in the Far East has been conducted. . . . In Australia, too, there is open criticism of the weakness of the Allied defences against the Japanese attack. Some Australians believe that we have grossly underestimated the relative importance of the Far East as compared with the other main theatres of the war'. In Berlin, such openness would probably have been dealt with by a firing squad.

Military success made the task of Allied propaganda much easier: Allied broadcasters and others were able to contrast the earlier boasts of

the Nazis with contemporary realities. In September 1942, for instance, Hitler had said: 'If I had an enemy of calibre—an enemy of military calibre—I could almost predict where he would strike. But when you are faced with military idiots . . .' Exactly a year later, the BBC commented: 'Military idiots. How does that sound today? It has a different meaning from a year ago. Today, when Italy has collapsed, when British and American troops stand on the mainland of Fortress Europe.' In the following two years the BBC, in its broadcasts to Europe, beat Goebbels at his own game. It refuted his claims, contrasted them with reality, mocked them. The monopoly of information in occupied Europe—the main objective of the 'uniformity' campaign early in the war—was broken. Although, in many occupied countries, listening to foreign broadcasts carried the death penalty, people went on listening to them. In the end, Goebbels even withdrew permits for monitoring foreign broadcasts from many high party and state departments.

In the closing stages of the war, Hitler became more and more withdrawn; he blamed the Germans for having betrayed him, and Goebbels had to carry the burden of trying to keep up their morale. He reached out for parallels into Germany's past; he made an all-out effort to divide the Western Allies from the Soviets. All this was without success. The last conference in the Ministry of Propaganda took place on 21 April 1945. Goebbels's theme was the treason committed by the old officers' clique against Hitler's Germany. A few days later both Hitler and Goebbels, and Goebbels's large family, were found dead by Red Army troops in a Berlin bunker.

There was a certain symmetry between the last stage of war-time propaganda in April 1945 and Goebbels's agitation in 1926. After he had

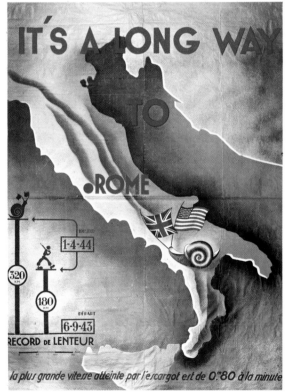

arrived in Berlin, Goebbels regarded himself as the man who wrested the capital of Germany from the local Communists; in 1945, he saw the capital fall to the Red Army. He was totally inexpert in military matters, and had perhaps overestimated the effectiveness of propaganda against the big battalions.

In the years between the outbreak of the First World War and the end of the Second—between 1914 and 1945—propaganda nevertheless moved to the forefront of the instruments available to the state for the pursuit of its aims. From modest beginnings, say, in Wellington House in London, under Charles Masterman's supervision, it became a big state industry. Vast sums of money were spent on it; thousands of people found employment in hundreds of propaganda organizations; it shaped the view of the world, and of its events, of millions. It became almost a respectable academic subject. Sociologists examined its organization and effectiveness, psychologists its links with education, marketing or religion.

Modern technology provided propaganda with new instruments which shaped the contents of propaganda. There was a leisurely, scholarly quality about the activities of Masterman; he still relied on the printed word exclusively and there were no daily deadlines for his pamphlets. The supreme importance of sound broadcasting in the Second World War introduced a hurried, almost breathless, note into the exchanges of the adversaries. The response had to be immediate in order to be effective; the airwaves resounded with continuous, sharp, sometimes ill-tempered argument.

The film was also harnessed into publicity for war for the first time. Newsreels were extremely popular everywhere in war-time; the Nazis had made a breakthrough in documentaries before the war, in particular with Leni Riefenstahl's filmed epics of the Nuremberg party rallies. There

Below and below right: Another German leaflet for the Allies on the beach-head at Anzio. The slow pace of the Allied conquest of Italy was ridiculed in many leaflets and posters.

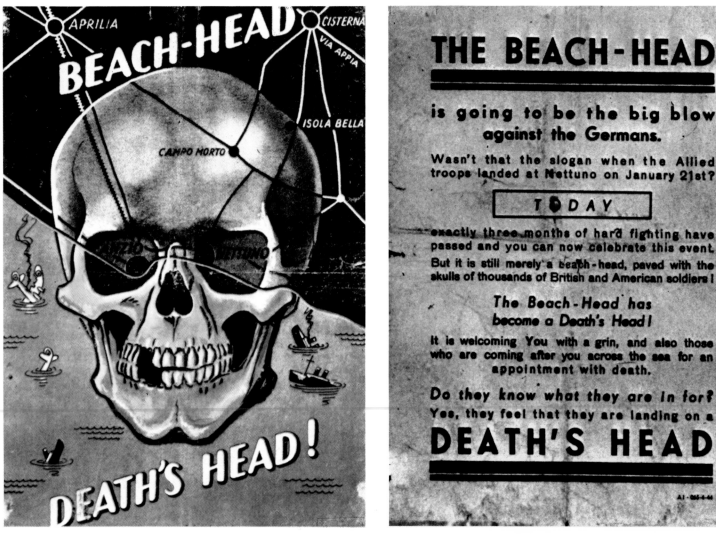

was a link between poster production and documentary film-making. The themes, for instance, of the 1932 poster 'National Socialism, the organized will of the nation' and of the film of one of the rallies, *Triumph of the Will*, were identical. But the various political experiments with feature films were less successful. The initial enthusiasm of Nazi film makers for putting across their message gradually evaporated. Perhaps their touch was too heavy, their message too ponderous. For instance, the hero of a film made before the war, Hitler Youth Quex, mercifully perished at the hands of Communist thugs. He was resurrected during the war, but now adult Pilot Quex became a figure of comedy rather than of high-minded drama. The public insisted on being amused rather than instructed.

Given the variety of propaganda media, and of the uses made of them, it was not surprising that posters came to play a lesser role in the Second than they had done in the First World War. In addition, a new form of product joined the poster sector of propaganda: the leaflet. The poster could be used by the governments only on their own territory or in the countries under their control. Some clandestine posters appeared in the occupied territories in Europe, but they were exceptions. Leaflets, on the other hand, were employed mainly against the enemy. They became one of the important instruments of psychological warfare; posters, in contrast, were employed on the home front.

The functions of leaflets were similar to those of posters: they informed, instructed, or suggested new ways of looking at the war. Their central ideas had to correspond to the mentality and the desires of their recipients; their appeal had to be easily comprehensible to the target audience. Their layout, like the layout of posters, had to conform to certain basic rules. It had to be striking, at once attracting attention; it had to draw attention in a certain direction, and in a certain sequence; its message had to be clear and capable of holding attention long enough for the message to sink in.

Like broadcasting, leaflets could be of the black, grey or white type, depending on their origin and degree of disguise. They could consist, like posters, mainly of text, but picture leaflets, as much as picture posters, were more popular with the propagandists because their visual message was more forceful and did not demand much intellectual effort on the part of the beholder. In addition, leaflets had two sides, whereas posters were of necessity one-sided. Text on one side and a picture or photograph on the other were one of the choices the makers of wartime leaflets could opt for. Postcards became a popular subdivision of this particular propaganda form.

As far as the text of the leaflets was concerned, it built on the theory that people seek out and understand information which corresponds to their wishes, expectations and needs; and that they ignore information which does not conform to those standards. There are, however, many examples of leaflets and posters which were downright offensive to their audiences. They can be largely traced to the early German activities in the occupied territories; they bullied, intimidated, threatened, often in a mockery of the native language. They are examples of the disregard of the 'master race' for its inferiors.

The most common means of dissemination of leaflets was by aircraft; early in the war, the crews simply threw them out of their planes in bundles. It was a time-consuming and imprecise method, and it wasted a lot of leaflets; on many occasions, too, the fuselage of the plane was damaged. The German *Propaganda-Atelier* in Berlin then developed the prop-bombs—tubes which could release the leaflets at a given height. In the summer of 1944, US Air Force Captain James Monroe then developed the 'Monroe bomb', which contained some 80,000 leaflets. In the course of one action, more than two million leaflets could hit the target. Towards the end of the war the Germans, and the countries occupied by them, came

STOP, WATCH YOUR STEP, IT'S FIVE MINUTES TO TWELVE!

5 Minutes to Twelve

Luftwaffe down and out.
German war industry smashed.
Russians threatening Berlin.
The end in sight.

5 Minutes to Twelve

And so nobody wants to be killed in these last five minutes. That's common sense.

Watch your step!

Top and above: One of the last German propaganda leaflets, designed to ensure complacency among the Western Allies. With the end in sight, no soldier wanted to be the last to die, but the speed of the Allied conquest did not slacken.

under saturation propaganda bombardment. In the last months of the war, the US 422nd Squadron alone released 1.5 billion leaflets; some 75,000 'Monroe bombs' had been produced before May 1945.

Even in comparison with the technological skill expended on the dissemination of leaflets—quite apart from the skill and expense used for other, more recent forms of propaganda—posters were simply the leaflets' poor relations. In terms of production, however, there were no great differences between the two forms of propaganda. Like posters, leaflets reached a high level of technical, and sometimes artistic, accomplishment. They played on the fears, desires and resentments of the enemy; many of them took the form of soft pornography. The Western Allies' leaflets to the German troops on the availability of German women, the lack of German men, and the presence of foreign workers in Germany carried a heavy punch; so did the German 'Life-Death' series, modelled on the cover page of *Life* magazine and distributed on the Italian front in October 1944.

Many of the posters and leaflets have survived, and even nowadays, more than three decades after the end of the war, many of them still succeed in evoking a particular period of the war, spelling out long-forgotten messages in a clear and direct language. Broadcasting scripts and tapes are at worst incomprehensible and at best informative. Propaganda films, especially feature films, have a similar anachronistic quality about them. Good newsreels, on the other hand, are documents of the time of their origin; they do not make any statement about that time. Posters and leaflets do make such statements, even in their least accomplished forms. They were usually created by individuals and not by large, anonymous teams; perhaps this is the reason why they have aged better than all the other artefacts of propaganda.

On the pages of this book, posters are divided into several groups according to their themes and irrespective of their country of origin. Within each group, the posters are normally arranged according to chronological sequence. The first group deals with posters making appeals to patriotism. They follow the First World War 'Your Country Needs You!' pattern, probably constituting the most important category for all countries. Secondly, there are the posters concerning national security. They instruct and exhort: people should keep their mouths shut because spies and saboteurs were around. Thirdly, there are the posters concerning the war effort. They are largely non-military; they deal with industrial production for the war, with government bonds and savings, with the mobilization of women. These first three groups make a direct appeal— the first and third groups positive, the second group negative—to the citizens. Then there are the alliance posters: how the two sides saw themselves, or each other, in terms of relations with their allies. Finally, there are the posters which make a statement about the enemy. It would now be difficult to make a quantitative analysis of their place in the overall poster production in each country, but it is my impression that the Germans in particular created more posters in this category than anyone else. They had, or thought they had, more enemies. There are, for example, the 'Red Menace' posters, mainly of German origin, which were often used in occupied Europe. They concerned Bolshevism and the threat it presented to European civilization. At many points, this group merges with the racist posters. Such posters have two main themes—anti-Semitism and *Untermensch* propaganda. The Slavs—the Russians in particular—were, in Nazi mythology, sub-human and ruled by a Jewish-Bolshevik clique. There was enough emotion, prejudice and fear in Hitler's Berlin, as well as conviction in the effectiveness of the message, to cause large numbers of these posters to be produced. The last section also contains the horror and atrocity posters—probably more popular, on both sides, in the First World War than in the Second, but still occasionally employed, especially in connection with the 'Red Menace' theme.

Right: Two of the most effective German leaflets, both using soft pornography in different ways. The top leaflet contrasts the allures of home and peace with the reality of war in 1944; the bottom one, produced early in the war, attempted to divide the Allies by its contrast of the beleaguered French poilu *with the high-living British serviceman who remained behind the lines.*

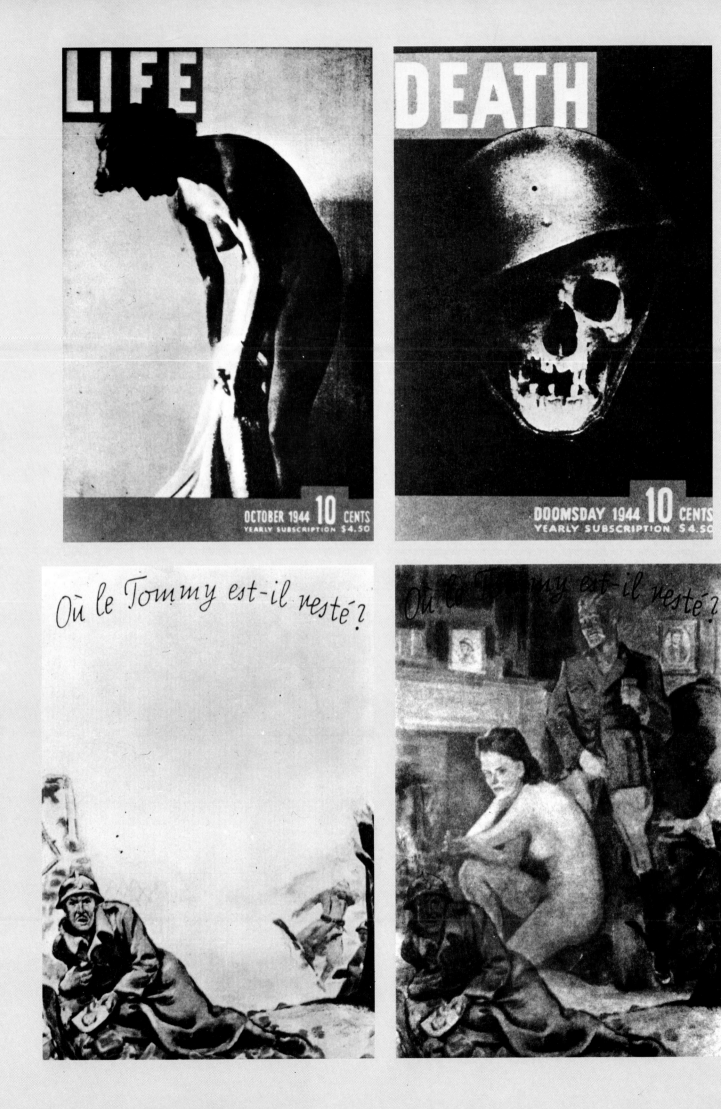

Your Country Needs You
The Appeal to Patriotism

Historians sometimes tend to see the Second World War as a continuation of the first, or to see the years 1914–45 as another Thirty Years War, a kind of long-drawn-out civil war in Europe. But the Second World War was neither a purely European war, nor was it fought out by civilians who were contesting political power in one state. It was fought largely by European states—by vast conscript armies in which professional soldiers were a minority. The soldier and the civilian were interchangeable; the whole nation had to be brought into the war effort, including women and, towards the end of the war in Germany, even children.

This 'total war' character of the Second World War meant that mass propaganda had to aim at the largest possible part of the population and convince it to be utterly loyal to the state. At the same time, the state was making demands on the people which, in peacetime, would have been intolerable. The strain must not lead to disloyalty, nor political doubt and dissent to treason; patriots had to defend their countries, to do their national duty, wherever required. Without such group loyalty the state could not have prosecuted the war.

Patriotic posters are therefore by far the largest group of wartime posters, and many of them make use of emotive symbols and emblems. National flags were of course the most popular of such devices, along with the swastika emblem on German posters, the hammer and sickle or the red star on Soviet posters. The French cross of Lorraine also appeared frequently.

Opposite: 'Victory Will be Ours!' This German poster by Zik was strongly influenced by the draftsmanship technique of Mjölnir (Hans Schweitzer). The poster incorporates the flag motif, common to many posters appealing to patriotism, as well as a blue-eyed, and probably fair-haired, soldier. His pure Aryan race does not prevent him from looking rather grim: the poster originated in 1942, when total war was about to become the order of the day.

These posters play on two psychological needs: the need for men and women to belong to a group, and the need for the group to have its own symbols, Flags, badges, banners, uniforms, colours—fashions in political symbols have often changed, but they can be traced to the beginnings of organized political life.

The heraldry of mediaeval and early modern European history was replaced by the flags and other insignia of modern nation-states. Many of the loyalty symbols used in the Second World War were of nineteenth-century origin. Others were more recently invented, or rediscovered after a long lapse of time. The red star and hammer and sickle of the Soviet state made their appearance soon after the revolution in 1917; the swastika emblem of the Nazis was an ancient emblem, probably a symbol of the sun. Kipling had used it before 1933 as a colophon in his books; Hitler chose it in the late 1920s as an emblem for his movement.

Such are the recurrent features of patriotic posters. Many of them are simply recruitment posters for the armed services, and sometimes the

'ARF A MO'

NATIONAL SERVICE NEEDS YOU

LEARN NOW!– BE READY!

Left: Bert Thomas's early (1939) ''Arf a Mo'' carried on the humorous school of posters which had been established by Thomas and Bruce Bairnsfather in Britain during the First World War. But the 'cartoon school' was more widely employed between 1939 and 1945 than in 1914–18, because it was realized in the Second World War that civilian morale needed an occasional tonic—constant appeals to patriotism might wear the patriots down.

Right: This French poster—'Join/Rejoin the Metropolitan Forces'—originated shortly before the war. It was a recruitment poster by Toussaint without the urgency and appeal of, say, the 'Your Country Needs You' type of poster. The two troops ignore the viewer, concentrating on the battlefield; it was a poster more suitable for peace than for war.

Page 34: Henri Guignon's 'Holding the Line' poster was published in America in 1942. It combined the head of Churchill with two patriotic symbols: the flag and the bulldog. Animal symbols—the Russian bear, the British bulldog—tended to lighten, even to humanize, the appeal of patriotic posters. The bulldog symbol was used in a British recruitment poster in the First World War; it had appeared as a symbol for Britain in a Russian print during the Napoleonic wars.

Page 35: 'We Will Return!' This Italian poster, produced after the surrender of the last Italian army in North Africa, expressed Mussolini's determination to regain his country's colonial empire. But it is not clear whether the large ghostly figure is meant to be the memory of the defeated armies, and the soldier in the foreground their avenger, or vice versa.

HOLDING the LINE!

RITORNEREMO!

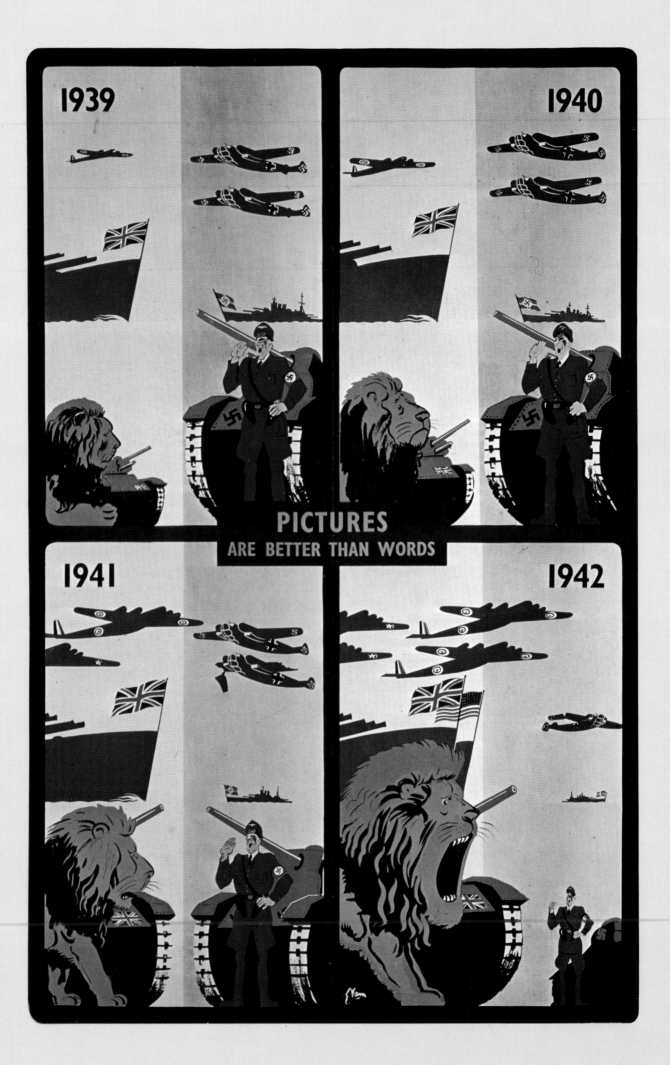

PICTURES
ARE BETTER THAN WORDS

Left: The British 1943 'Pictures are Better than Words' poster used a simplified strip-cartoon technique. It was meant to illustrate the relative strengths of British and German armed forces over the years 1939–42. Again, the animal symbol—this time the lion—is used, and its variations are probably the most effective feature of an otherwise rather ineffective poster. The alliance theme—the US flag and aircraft markings—makes an unostentatious entry into the last segment of the poster.

Right: Mjölnir—Hans Schweitzer was his proper name—embodied the spirit and the aspirations of the Nazis in his drawings more effectively than any other contemporary German artist. He specialized in images of iron-jawed storm-troopers; his famous 1932 election poster 'National Socialism, the Organized Will of the Nation' had the profiles of three such storm-troopers superimposed on each other. In comparison his wartime recruitment poster for the SS, 'You Can Join Them on Your 17th Birthday', lacked some of the brutality of his pre-war stylized thugs. The small patriotic motif in the background—the Nazi standard—was based on a design by Hitler himself.

Page 38: The German poster 'New Europe is Invincible' was published sometime in 1942, and was perhaps the most informative poster the Nazis produced during the war. It gives prominence to a graphic account of German military operations; the smaller insert in the top right-hand corner gives an account of the 'enemy plans' in 1939. The text gives a six-point programme, attributed to 'British plutocrats, their American allies, and the Jewish string-pullers'. All their evil plans were frustrated, including point six: the Bolshevik steam-roller (echoing the memory of the First World War 'Russian steam-roller') was meant to destroy the German people. The poster has to be read, and for that reason alone it fails as a poster.

Page 39: 'One Fight, One Victory!' celebrates the tenth anniversary of Hitler becoming the Chancellor of the German Reich. It is another variation by Mjölnir on his iron-jaws theme. The SA man in the background reflects the Nazi theory that the party's struggle and the state's were one.

state emblems and symbols are repeated on the uniforms worn by the men and women portrayed on the posters; and on other posters the colours or the symbols of the national flags are employed in a variety of permutations. The poster commemorating the tenth anniversary of the Nazi regime on 30 January 1943, made by the veteran Nazi poster painter Mjölnir, is a good example of this technique. An earlier wartime poster, 'Victory Will be Ours', makes the same point by the employment of a similar technique. Henri Guignon's poster with the head of Churchill on the body of a bulldog, against the background of the Union Jack and with the slogan 'Holding the Line!', makes the point of dogged determination in contrast to the German posters of pure optimism.

The main movements of wartime propaganda and the changes in the fortunes of war are reflected in the posters dealing with patriotic themes. This is illustrated by the two German posters referred to above. From the point of view of technique there is little difference between them. But in the earlier poster the grim, blue-eyed *Wehrmacht* trooper looks forward—rather passively—to the inevitable victory. The second poster, 'One Fight, One Victory!', appeared soon after Goebbels had launched his 'total war' campaign. It has a dynamic quality absent from the other

Das Programm der britischen Plutokraten, ihrer amerikanischen Bundesgenossen und der jüdischen Drahtzieher:

① Polen mußte den Kriegsbrand entfachen.

② Norwegen sollte als Sprungbrett für einen Stoß in die ungeschützte Nordflanke des Reiches dienen.

③ Durch Holland und Belgien hindurch sollten die Franzosen und die übrigen Hilfsvölker Groß-

britanniens in das deutsche Industriegebiet und damit in das Herz des Deutschen Reiches eindringen.

④ Im Süden sollte Italien aus Nordafrika hinausgeschlagen und als »Gefangener des Mittelmeeres« als aktiver Bundesgenosse Deutschlands ausgeschaltet werden.

⑤ Die Balkanländer Griechenland und Jugoslawien waren als Aufmarschgebiete für eine Front im Südosten ausersehen.

⑥ Als letzter großer Vernichtungsschlag sollte dann schließlich die gigantische bolschewistische Dampfwalze über das deutsche Volk, alles zerstörend, hinwegbrausen.

Alle diese Pläne sind gescheitert! Jeder neue Versuch eines Angriffs endete mit einer neuen Niederlage für unsere Gegner.

Nach drei Jahren Krieg stehen die den Achsenmächten angeschlossenen jungen Nationen Europas geschlossen und siegreich gegen eine zusammenbrechende plutokratisch-bolschewistische Front.

Das neue Europa ist unschlagbar

РОДИНА-МАТЬ ЗОВЕТ!

ВОЕННАЯ ПРИСЯГА

Я, гражданин Союза Советских Социалистических Республик, вступая в ряды Рабоче-Крестьянской Красной Армии, принимаю присягу и торжественно клянусь быть честным, храбрым, дисциплинированным, бдительным бойцом, строго хранить военную и государственную тайну, беспрекословно выполнять все воинские уставы и приказы командиров и начальников.

Я клянусь добросовестно изучать военное дело, всемерно беречь военное и народное имущество и до последнего дыхания быть преданным своему Народу, своей Советской Родине и Рабоче-Крестьянскому Правительству.

Я всегда готов по приказу Рабоче-Крестьянского Правительства выступить на защиту моей Родины — Союза Советских Социалистических Республик и, как воин Рабоче-Крестьянской Красной Армии, я клянусь защищать ее мужественно, умело, с достоинством и честью, не щадя своей крови и самой жизни для достижения полной победы над врагами.

Если же по злому умыслу я нарушу эту мою торжественную присягу, то пусть меня постигнет суровая кара советского закона, всеобщая ненависть и презрение трудящихся.

Left: Irakly Toidze's Soviet poster 'Your Mother-Country Appeals to You!' appeared soon after the German invasion of Russia in 1941. The female figure representing the mother-country holds the text of the Russian military oath in her hand; the background of bayonets is simple and effective.

poster; even the flags underscore that quality. More importantly, it symbolizes the unity between the party and the state in the two figures portrayed on it.

On the whole, patriotic posters have little place for humour. Their message is grand, sometimes pompous; exclamation marks at the end of slogans are frequent. The British poster ''Arf a Mo', National Service Needs You' is an exception, but it had appeared before the introduction of compulsory service in April 1939 and before the outbreak of the war.

There is an element of grim 'gallows humour' in some of the Soviet posters; the 'New Year' poster has that element. Nevertheless, the Soviet posters represented in this group reflect a major propaganda switch. For instance, the 'We Shall Defend the Gains of October!' poster, a reply to the

Above: There was some initial hesitation in Soviet propaganda between the straight patriotic appeal, illustrated by the poster at left, and the patriotic appeal underscored by ideology as seen in this one, 'We Shall Defend the Gains of October', i.e. of the October 1917 revolution. On the whole, the Soviets opted for the straight patriotic appeal.

Right: The 'Happy New Year' poster contains the juxtaposition of the Red Army soldier, his head surrounded by stars, and the dreadful German troops trying to celebrate the coming of the New Year 1943. Soviet poster technique tended to be very direct in its appeal, and rather unflattering to the enemy. Though Soviet political graphic art did not have the large hinterland of commercial advertising to fall back on, it had a long and distinguished school of poster-painting.

This page: The US posters seen here use three distinct techniques. There is the patriotic-historical appeal of the first poster, where the troops of the War of Independence are linked with the US troops of 1943: the contemporary soldiers turn their 'eyes right' to their historical tradition. The Civilian Defense poster uses the animal symbol, though the eagle here is used in a rather ambivalent manner. C.D. was really air defence, but the eagle is obviously attacking. McClelland Barclay's action-drawing 'Let 'em Have It' is a recruitment poster for the US Navy. The action-painting school was popular with US wartime graphic artists, and owed a great deal to photography.

German invasion, refers to the Bolshevik revolution of 1917 and to the socialist achievement. But other Soviet posters, and Soviet propaganda, concentrated on the non-political patriotic theme. The military oath poster, for instance—'Mother-Country Appeals to You!'—is a good example of the transition to patriotic appeal.

The US posters often add freedom to patriotism as an element which must be defended. In this way, they make a simple ideological point about the war which—perhaps with the exception of the Soviet 'Gains of October' poster—is almost wholly absent from European posters issued in the Allied interest. There are posters which summarize the progress of the war: the British poster 'Pictures are Better than Words' uses the strip-cartoon technique, in four parts, to give a simple and satisfactory 'progress report' up to the year 1942. For the same year, the German poster 'The New Europe is Invincible' makes the same point in an entirely different way. It shows Germany's gains and the geography of the new Nazi and Nazi-occupied Europe—the development of 'Fortress Europe'.

The frightened faces of the old and the young man on the recruitment poster for the *Volkssturm*—the last-minute people's defence army—show the decline of Germany's military power and of poster draftsmanship. It may be contrasted with the joyful quality of the 1945 French poster, created by Hansi in Epinal, a town famous for its military prints, or with the Soviet poster 'We Shall Fly the Flag of Victory over Berlin!'

Left: This French poster, probably published after the fall of France in one of the Western Allied countries, used the patriotic symbols simply and effectively. The graffiti formula suggests popular resistance against Nazi occupation, and that the painter of the patriotic graffiti was in a bit of a hurry.

Opposite: This poster by Hansi of Epinal celebrates the end of the war, the defeat of the Germans, and the Western wartime alliance. Its cheerful cartoon quality is underscored by the memory of the gallows, very much in the background of the picture.

Left: This German People's Defence poster was drawn by Mjölnir, in his customary style. But the old and the young man's jaws are no longer made of pure iron; is it fear or determination in their eyes? The Volkssturm was the last-ditch defence force; it fought for 'freedom' and mainly for 'life', and little else.

Page 46: Mjölnir used the same theme of grim, last-ditch determination in this 'Front-line Town Frankfurt will be Held' Poster. Women, old men and children had to defend their homes, destroyed in air raids. This was one of the last posters produced in Nazi Germany, and it clearly marks the end of an era.

Page 47: In contrast, the Soviet poster, like the Hansi poster, is full of jubilation. 'We Shall Fly the Flag of Victory over Berlin' celebrates the Allied victory, but leaves the viewer in no doubt as to who played the major role in that victory, and who would be first in Berlin.

ВОДРУЗИМ НАД БЕРЛИНОМ ЗНАМЯ ПОБЕДЫ!

You Never Know Who's Listening
Beating the Spies and Saboteurs

The government's view of the security of the state and of the measures required for its maintenance affects the whole temper of life in the state. If the government sees the state as being beleaguered by enemies, external or internal, it then has to take appropriate measures. These include intelligence and internal security organizations, secret police, and covert operations of one kind or another.

Between the two wars, the liberal democracies of the West concentrated on the gathering of military intelligence and on protecting their own secrets, and left it at that. The one-party states, on the other hand, in particular under Hitler and Stalin, ran complex and powerful security organizations. Then, after the outbreak of the war, internal security, like propaganda, was an activity which had to be taken care of by the state. In all the belligerent countries the military and civilian security services were greatly expanded and their aim became clear-cut. They had to protect the home front and the army, the whole war effort of their countries, against the internal enemy.

Concern with national security and patriotic enthusiasm; appeals to people to keep their mouths shut and to fight hard against the enemy—they are two sides of the same coin. But the appeal to group loyalty, to patriotism, is a positive appeal; concern with national security is a matter of warning. The designers of security posters were therefore faced with a much harder task than the designers of patriotic posters. They had no immediately recognizable symbols to fall back on, unless they used the

Opposite: The US poster 'Award for Careless Talk' was constructed by Stevan Dohanos for the Office of War Information in 1944. One of the best-known American posters dealing with national security, it made skilful use of enemy symbols: an appeal to patriotism in reverse.

CARELESS TALK
...got there first

symbols of the enemy. Such a technique aimed to draw the people's attention to the danger from the other side—a way of making posters which needs careful handling. This technique was used, with some success, in the American poster 'Award for Careless Talk'. It is a striking poster, but it requires a swift double-take on the part of the viewer before the message reaches home.

The poster designers who tackled the theme of national security simply had to be more inventive than the designers of other types of poster; they certainly experimented more, with some remarkable results. Photomontage and cartoons were the two preferred techniques; the customary drawn or painted posters could fall very flat indeed. The two conventional American posters, for instance, 'Careless Talk ... Got There First', and the hauntingly sentimental '... Because Somebody Talked!' can hardly be called hard-hitting. The ultimate outcome and the cause—careless talk—were not graphically linked, and the technical execution of the posters was inadequate. The blend of blurred photograph, geometrical design, and drawing in the 'Your Talk May Kill your Comrades' poster is direct in its message and effect; and the 'Keep it Dark, Careless Talk Costs Lives' poster is similarly effective.

Most of the national security posters were concerned with the effect of information leakage on the military effort; a few pinpointed the effect of sabotage on war industry. The US cartoon 'Watch for this Guy!' equated sabotage with treason and the civilian war-production worker with the soldier. But the designer of the poster found it necessary to provide his message with, for a poster, a long explanatory text. In 'The Saboteur's Favorite Weapon is Arson', a specific form of sabotage was pinpointed.

Whether they made appeals on behalf of military or war-industry security, the posters firmly concentrated on the enemy within; they pointed, in the same way as the patriotic posters, to the need for national unity. In a way, they encouraged a mild form of mass paranoia—the feeling that the state was being besieged, and not only from the outside but also from 'the enemy within'.

a careless word

...another cross

...because somebody talked!

THE SABOTEUR'S FAVORITE WEAPON IS *arson*

SABOTEUR (MEANING TRAITOR)

He's a Snake in the Grass, he strikes without warning, he's smooth, he's slick, he's the king of Double-Crossers, he works in the Light, he wrecks in the Dark, he's the monkey-wrench in the machinery, the emery dust in the oil . . . he's the Judas of Democracy. *Watch For Him . . . .*

★ ★ ★

You are a **PRODUCTION SOLDIER**...
America's First Line of Defense is HERE

REMEMBER PEARL HARBOR

FIFTH COLUMN

The Jap Snake struck hard because it was helped by dirty inside work -- Don't kid yourself . . . It *CAN* happen here! Keep your Eyes Open and your Ears Cocked . . . Report *ANYTHING* that looks queer.

You are a **PRODUCTION SOLDIER**...
America's First Line of Defense is HERE

This page: The posters here illustrate the difficulties faced in the making of security posters. They had no immediately recognizable symbols to fall back on; they had to explain the points they were trying to make in the text, and in the inscriptions on their cartoon figures. Gino Bocasili's Italian poster of 1943, 'Keep Quiet, the Enemy is Listening' (right) is, in contrast, more effective: it makes a simpler visual impact. So are the German and Finnish security posters (pages 54 and 55): the German poster concerns black-out, a modern problem which is treated in an almost mediaeval manner.

Stärk fronten här hemma-

Bygg dammar för ryktena !

Starve him with Silence

WAR Secrets

'706

THIS POSTER IS PUBLISHED BY THE HOUSE OF SEAGRAM AS PART OF ITS CONTRIBUTION TO THE NATIONAL VICTORY EFFORT

BEWARE

TROOP TRAIN WRECKED BLAME CARELESS TALK

THE WALLS HAVE EARS

jac leonard

ISSUED BY WARTIME INFORMATION BOARD, OTTAWA. PRINTED IN CANADA   DESIGN, COURTESY WALLS HAVE EARS ORGANIZATION

This page: Again, diverse security posters, groping for a technique, and for a clear-cut symbol. In contrast, 'Your Talk May Kill Your Comrades' (opposite), designed by Abram Games and published early in 1942, used a supremely effective technique. This was one of the most famous wartime posters, by one of the best-known British poster-painters. Games, the son of a photographer, was born in London in 1914. He won a poster competition prize in 1935, and became, in 1942, the official War Office poster designer. Games's approach to poster-making was hard-hitting and unsentimental; he used bold, unusual lettering, photomontage, striking colours. His posters—he made about a hundred of them during the war—carried a simple message, and Games believed all the points he made in his posters; shortly after the war he wrote that 'I feel strongly that the high purpose of wartime posters was mainly responsible for their excellence'.

LOOK WHO'S Listening

'705   THIS POSTER IS PUBLISHED BY THE HOUSE OF SEAGRAM AS PART OF ITS CONTRIBUTION TO THE NATIONAL VICTORY EFFORT

S'long Dad! We're shiftin' to... *Blimey, I nearly said it!*

Left: 'Careless Talk Costs Lives' also used the photomontage technique, but with less effect. An entirely different way of presenting the same slogan—the cartoon poster (below) drawn by Fougasse (Cyril Kenneth Bird) in 1940—cut the subject down to human size. Bird was Art Editor of Punch *from 1937–48, and Editor from 1948–53. He had joined the Royal Engineers in 1914; his pseudonym, Fougasse, was the name of a small land mine, used only by the Royal Engineers, which sometimes hit the target.*

CARELESS TALK COSTS LIVES

Above: Bruce Bairnsfather, the artist who designed 'Even the Walls . . .' was, like Bird, wounded in the First World War, and when he recuperated he was attached to the Intelligence Department as an officer-cartoonist. He served in the 1939–45 war as a cartoonist attached to the US Army in Europe. His poster, however, does not have the punch and the simplicity of Bird's drawing, nor the technical accomplishment of Games's design.

'Talk Kills' was another poster on the security theme by Abram Games; the French poster by Paul Colin 'Silence, l'Enemie . . .' (right) also tackled this difficult theme with imagination and a touch of humour. The enemy was the sinister figure in the shadowy background: the friends were the innocent, slightly comic civilian and military figures who clearly had no idea how secret was the information which the state had entrusted to them.

SILENCE

PAUL COLIN

L'ENNEMI..
GUETTE VOS CONFIDENCES

Back Them Up
The Campaign for War Production

In a war in which civilians could change places with soldiers at short notice, the links between the home front and the military fronts were very close. In any case, the distinction between the civilian hinterland and the front line was becoming blurred. Many towns and industries of the nations at war were within the reach of enemy aircraft and their bombs.

The strategists of the First World War were confounded by the 'element of technological surprise' in several ways. They had planned for a war of fast movement consisting of short, sharp campaigns. In fact, the Western Front—the theatre of war with the highest level of technological accomplishment on both sides—became bogged down in a warfare of attrition. Massed infantry attacks dissolved in the face of modern armaments; the machine gun, with its sweeping line of fire, dominated the field. The military planners also consistently underestimated their requirements for armaments, and for shells in particular. The Second World War, on the other hand, straightaway became what the first war was supposed to have been. The technology and strategy of the tank weapon, the main vehicle of movement in the Second World War, had been developed; supported by fully motorized infantry, with adequate air cover, it became unbeatable in the opening stages of the war.

The links between the factory and the front line, between the war effort and the supporting technology, had been established; soldiers were becoming mechanics, as well as fighters. Nor were the armies of the Second World War constantly hampered by the underproduction of armaments.

Opposite: The war-effort posters were the most sharply defined group of World War II posters. Fighting became more a matter of technology than of heroism in the course of the military engagements of the second half of the nineteenth century; the 'element of technological surprise' slowed down fighting on the Western front in 1914–18 to a war of attrition. Technology had to be underpinned by finance: the point is illustrated in this early Second World War French poster, 'Subscribe to Armament Bonds'.

For instance, it has been estimated that, in the few weeks between 22 June 1941 and the end of August, Soviet losses amounted to over 5,000 aircraft. The Germans started then writing off the Soviet Air Force as a fighting weapon. But reinforcements kept on coming in. What the Soviet Air Force lacked in quality—slower, less manoeuvreable aircraft, light bomb-loads, virtual absence of ground control—they made up, in the opening stages of the war, in numbers. Russian aircraft production had started outstripping German production in 1937; it rose from 800 a month to 900 in 1938, and about 1,000 at the time of Hitler's invasion of the USSR. Deliveries from new factories in the Urals had started reaching the air force in 1939; after initial setbacks, Soviet aircraft production recovered in mid-1942, and then rose to an amazing 3,000 a month. In the second half of the war, the Soviets surpassed German aircraft production in terms of quality as well. Improvements in all sectors were so rapid that the Germans did not believe them possible. But at the same time, Allied strategists also took note of the amazing flexibility of German war production in the most difficult conditions under massive Allied air attacks.

Right: Yvonne Roger's appeal for money to back up the French army, 'He Watches, He Will Win'.

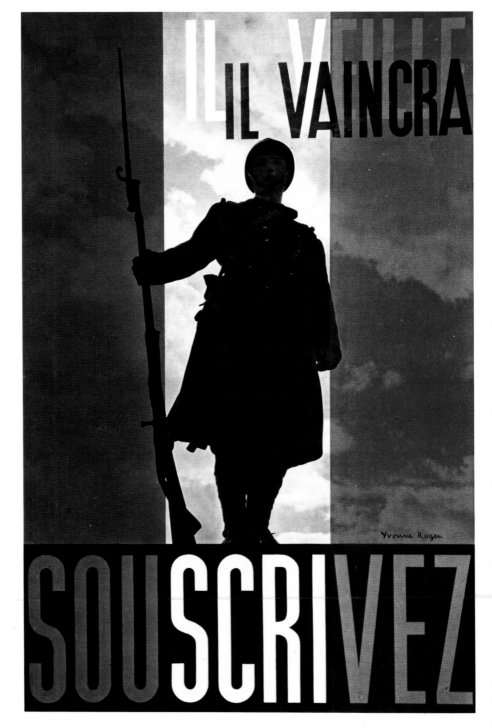

SCHRIJFT IN OP DE

ONAFHANKELIJKHEIDS-LEENING

VEILIGHEID VEILIGHEID

schrijft in op de

ONAFHANKELIJKHEIDS-LEENING

Nevertheless, sometime in the Second World War Europe started losing its primacy as the armaments workshop of the world. It lost it to America, and in the process America itself became transformed. Its Gross National Product rose from $91bn to $166bn during the war, and industrial output was doubled. In terms of war production, this meant the expansion of US shipbuilding from 1m tons to 19m tons a year, of aircraft production from below 6,000 a year in 1941 to over 96,000. The number of people employed in the aircraft industry rose from 46,000 to over 2m. Of the 275,000 US-built aircraft, some 40,000 were sent to America's allies. Tank production increased to 14,000 in 1942 and 21,000 in 1943. US industry produced 64,000 landing craft, compared with 4,300 made in Britain. Of their vast jeep production, the Americans were able to spare 86,000 for the British. In addition, America supplied the Soviet Union with goods worth $11.3bn and Britain with £428m: 22,000 aircraft, 13,000 tanks, whole oil refinery plants, and so on. According to post-war Soviet estimates, Western aid accounted for 4% of Soviet production during the war; Western estimates differ, and are higher.

Such a tremendous war effort required as forceful a mobilization of manpower as mobilization for the armed forces did. The posters in this group closely resemble those appealing to patriotism, but they are more specialized and are aimed at the civilian population. Generally, they stress the parallel between the front-line soldier and the factory worker, and point to the dependence of the soldier on the worker. They often appeal on behalf of production for the individual services, and many of them establish the connection between financial sacrifice (taking the form of war bonds) and war production. Indeed, the US Treasury Department was one of the most active sponsors of this group of posters.

This page: Two Flemish posters produced before the German invasion in 1940, asking Belgians to contribute in order to preserve the nation's borders against foreign aggression.

WOMEN OF BRITAIN
COME INTO THE FACTORIES
ASK AT ANY EMPLOYMENT EXCHANGE FOR ADVICE AND FULL DETAILS

British field-guns smash a German tank attack at point-blank range in Libya

BACK THEM UP!

Again, these posters were not as difficult to design as the posters in the national security group. Their objective was clear and simple; their appeal had to be positive; in their execution, they had to stress the technological nature of the war. This point was made very simply in the early French wartime poster 'Souscrivez aux Bons d'Armament': the tanks are being overflown by massed aircraft, with a small flag to identify the leading tank. But war production meant, in the first place, labour recruitment: manpower was being replaced or extended by womanpower, and new employment offices were being set up in order to mobilize labour. The British poster appeals to women to come into factories; the American poster 'Labour: Step into This Picture' underscores the point of national unity by stressing the dependence of the armed services on labour.

On the whole, the US war-effort posters emphasize very strongly the patriotic nature of such effort; the Americans probably produced more posters of this type than anyone else. The series of war-bonds posters provides good examples. First there is the 'To Have and to Hold' poster, which is on the borderline between our first and third group of posters: it simply equates war bonds with patriotism. The grim appeal of 'War Bonds are Cheaper than Wooden Crosses' makes its own gloomy point; the design of the Victory Loan poster, with the shadowy President Roosevelt in the background, reaches out for a near-religious message. That message is put across in full in the 'Strong in the Strength of the Lord' poster: an unusual point to make in the Second World War, though more customary in the first.

Above left: The 'Women of Britain, Come into the Factories' poster illustrates the contribution women could make to the war effort, while the 'Back Them Up!' (above) and 'When? It's up to You!' (right) posters point to the importance of the production workers in the war. Harold Pym's poster 'Back Them Up!' used the action-picture technique, which we have noticed especially in connection with the design of US posters; the 'When?' poster contrasts bloodied Hitler with massed British aircraft. It slightly exaggerates the importance of workers in industry, and indicates that the length of the war depended on their effort.

Railways are the link between the Factories and Fighting Services

RAILWAY EQUIPMENT
IS
WAR EQUIPMENT

In contrast, the Soviet posters concentrate on war production alone. Money does not play a dynamic role in Soviet economy; its role is that of an accounting unit, a way of keeping the score rather than of influencing the game. Therefore there are no war bonds or other 'financial' posters; 'More Metal means More Armaments' is the simple message of the worker to the workers.

In the West, and especially in America, this group of posters creates a link between commercial advertising and political propaganda. Appeals for money and the stress on the role of industry in the war are themes which are not at the centre of patriotism; design techniques therefore show considerable variations, and patriotic symbols are employed rarely. When such symbols are used as in the 'To Have and to Hold' poster on page 73 they do not make for effective propaganda.

Above: Technical capability is aptly illustrated in Jean Carlu's design entitled 'America's Answer! Production'. The poster proves that modern design is best suited to publicize the key features of modern warfare.

Strong in the strength of the land
we who fight in the people's cause
will never stop until that cause is won

Left: David Stone Martin, in his 1942 poster made for the US Office of War Information, used a religious text together with a secular picture: the two features of the poster create a melodramatic effect which is not diminished by the main theme of the illustration: the unity between the civilian and the fighting population.

Below: A more restrained poster illustrating the same theme.

Right: This US poster, like the British 'When?' poster (page 66), intimates that the day of victory can be brought nearer by greater sacrifice—in this case financial—on the home front.

Pages 72–3: The war bond theme was taken up again in a series of posters issued by the US Treasury. Their themes and draftsmanship again cross the border into melodrama. Human sentiment is appealed to in the poster which maintains that wooden crosses are more expensive than war bonds; patriotic sentiment, and a patriotic symbol, dominate the 'To Have and to Hold!' poster.

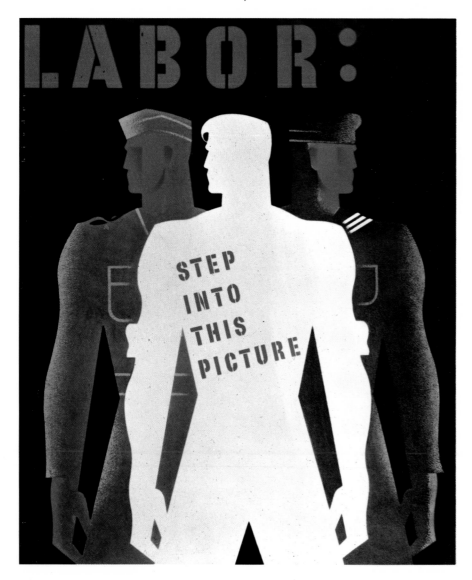

"In the strength of great hope we must shoulder our common load."

BUY VICTORY BONDS

VICTORY LOAN

Left: The religious symbolism of this poster is strong, but implicit; the head of President Roosevelt floating above the text in Gothic lettering, lettering sometimes associated with the word of God; the cross and the family, seen from the back and facing a better tomorrow; taken together, these features must have oversold Victory Bonds.

Left: This 1940 poster from the Atelier Albrecht publicized charitable collections for the 'Winter War Aid' campaign. The poster features the strong German profiles and the dynamic optimism of the early months of the war.

Above: 'The Italian Woman, by her renunciations and her sacrifices, marches along with the fighting men.'

Page 76: The Wehrmacht soldier exhorts the worker to work for victory as bravely as he was, visibly, fighting.

Page 77: W. Petzold's poster advised the civilians to save gas for the armaments industry.

Spare Gas
für die
RÜSTUNG

Below: Soviet poster-painters at least did
not have to bother with the financial
aspects of the war; the Soviets had no war
bonds, and they concentrated on the purely
technical aspects of the war. This poster
stated that more metal meant more
armaments.

Right: This appeal asked the production
workers to supply the Red Army with
more arms, adding 'Everything for the
Front!' in its main caption.

United We Are Strong
The International Crusade

The Second World War started in the East of Europe, over Poland: Hitler's Germany and Poland were the first belligerent states. Britain and France came into the war two days after the invasion of Poland, on 3 September 1939. The calm of the 'phony war' in the West was broken by the German invasion of Denmark and Norway in April 1940; in May the Low Countries were invaded; France was knocked out of the war when the German armies entered Paris in June 1940 and the armistice was signed on 22 June. Italy declared war on 10 June 1940; the Tripartite Pact between Germany, Italy and Japan was signed on 27 September. It was joined by Hungary, Romania and Slovakia two months later. By then, the Italians had invaded Egypt on 14 September 1940 and Greece on 28 October. Bulgaria and Yugoslavia joined the Tripartite Pact in March 1941; a month later, the Germans came into Yugoslavia and Greece. After the short-lived Soviet-Nazi pact, the Germans invaded the USSR on 22 June 1941; on 7 December Japan attacked Pearl Harbor, the Philippines, Hong Kong and Malaya, and sent a declaration of war to the US. The war had become global, and the main dividing lines between the alliances had been laid down.

In Europe, the pattern of the First World War alliances—the East and the West against the centre—was repeated, but with important differences in subsequent developments. In the First World War, the West managed to hold its ground against the Germans in France; Tsarist Russia, on the other hand, was defeated. In the Second World War, France

Opposite: This Soviet poster illustrated the sentence 'The Red Army with the armies of our Allies will break the back of the Fascist beast' in a speech by Stalin. Drawn partly in the form of a cartoon, the poster was designed to promote the Anglo-American-Soviet alliance; it also depicted the beastliness of the enemy, and contrasted it with the determination of the Soviets and their Allies.

ANGLIO! TWOJE DZIEŁO!

Above: An early German poster, issued for the benefit of the Poles. It states flatly 'England, This is Your Work!'—the words of a rather battered Polish soldier to a British politician, probably Chamberlain. The political intention of the poster was to undermine enemy alliances.

swiftly collapsed and the German armies came to a halt on the English Channel; the Soviets, on othe other hand, managed to reverse, after hard and costly fighting, their early setbacks.

After the Allied landings and advance in Italy, that nation got rid of Mussolini and switched sides, declaring war on Germany on 13 October 1943. On 6 June 1944 the Allies landed in Normandy; two days before, the Americans had entered Rome. By then the Red Army had begun its recovery of lost territory, advancing towards the German border and Berlin. There was little doubt then about the ultimate outcome of the war; the question was how long the dissolution and defeat of the Tripartite Pact would take.

The immensely complex military and diplomatic development of the war, which is very briefly sketched here, caused an enormous variety of posters to be produced. In the first place, there was the simple message of the posters outlining the alliances. Here, the Soviet posters are the most clear-cut and informative. For instance the poster illustrating Stalin's sentence 'The Red Army, with the Armies of our Allies, will Break the Back of the Fascist Beast' puts across the alliance theme simply and credibly. It is, in fact, a variation on patriotic posters, extending the theme to include the country's friends.

Many people from occupied Europe found a refuge in Britain. They joined the armed forces, or their own units within the British forces; joined the BBC and established and ran their national sections within the corporation; set up governments or national councils. They contested the loyalty of the people left behind with the local (usually collaborationist) government and with its masters, the Germans. There are, for instance, the Vichy government posters in this section, as well as the posters produced in London by General de Gaulle's Free French. For instance, the

THE BRITISH COMMONWEALTH OF NATIONS

TOGETHER

'La Victoire des Nations Unies est Maintenant Certaine' poster makes the same point, and in a similar way, as the Soviet poster. The poster honouring the F.F.I.—*Forces Françaises de l'Interieur* or resistance against the Germans—also chose the alliance theme.

On the other hand, the poster for occupied France, 'La Puissance de l'Allemagne Garante de sa Victoire', makes precisely the opposite point, in a sombre way. It warns the French that there is no point in resisting the Germans; the Germans are too strong. It is a good example of the propaganda of stark power.

On the British and American side we have a number of posters designed to promote knowledge about their less-well-known or smaller allies: Greece, Yugoslavia, Czechoslovakia, Holland. The Poles are represented here as well: the 'We do not Beg for Freedom, We Fight for It' poster was a reminder of the continued Polish participation in the war, within Poland as well as outside.

All these exiled peoples were concentrated on an island off the coast of occupied Europe. They were easy to reach, and they were on the whole united in their purpose: to rid their countries of the Germans. The Germans, on the other hand, were, at the half-way point of the war, in possession of the best part of Europe. Their lines of communications were vastly extended; in many places they faced hostile, or at least sullen, populations. They had to use terror and propaganda in order to sustain their thinly spread power; but there were several reasons why they were often frustrated in their purpose. Their ideology, we have noted, was an empty shell; they saw themselves as the master race and were reluctant to ask for assistance, especially from 'inferior' peoples. And their treatment of the native populations, especially in the East of Europe, was not calculated to gain them many friends. Nevertheless, they made the

Above: Another poster on the theme of cohesion of an alliance. The British Commonwealth of Nations was shown to be in the war together, against the background of the Union Jack. It is interesting to note that the draftsman of the poster discarded the imperial in favour of the commonwealth theme.

attempt. The series of posters on behalf of the *Waffen* SS are in fact recruitment posters for the Aryans; their Nordic, pure-race appeal is intensified especially in the case of Denmark and Norway, though such posters were issued for the benefit of the Dutch, the Belgians and the French as well. There was even an attempt (almost entirely unsuccessful) to recruit British prisoners of war into the SS in the last few months of the war.

There is another group of Nazi posters, aimed at the population of the occupied Slav countries in East Europe. The poster issued in Poland, 'Britain, This is Your Work!' aimed to divide the Poles from their allies in the West; the poster for the occupied Soviet territory 'The Might of Germany Grows Every Day' again uses, without any embellishments, the theme of stark power.

Though there is a solitary poster, aimed at the French, which portrays the *Wehrmacht* as a welfare organization which takes care of abandoned children, such posters were rarely attempted. The designers of Nazi posters found the theme, say, of the Jewish international conspiracy against pure German gentiles easier to handle.

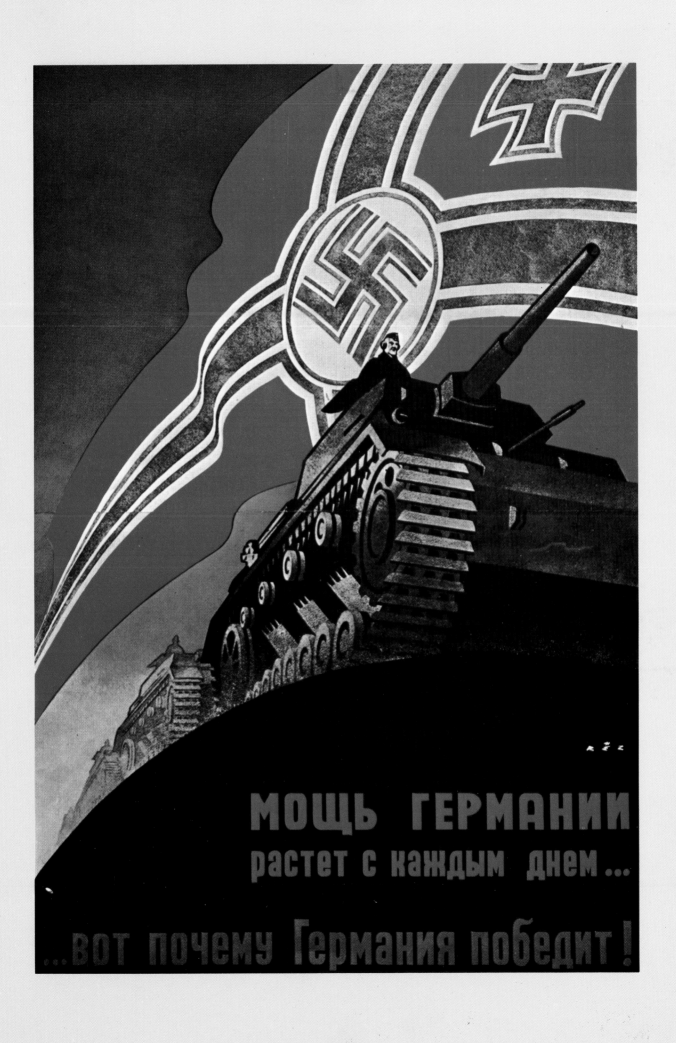

МОЩЬ ГЕРМАНИИ
растет с каждым днем...

...вот почему Германия победит!

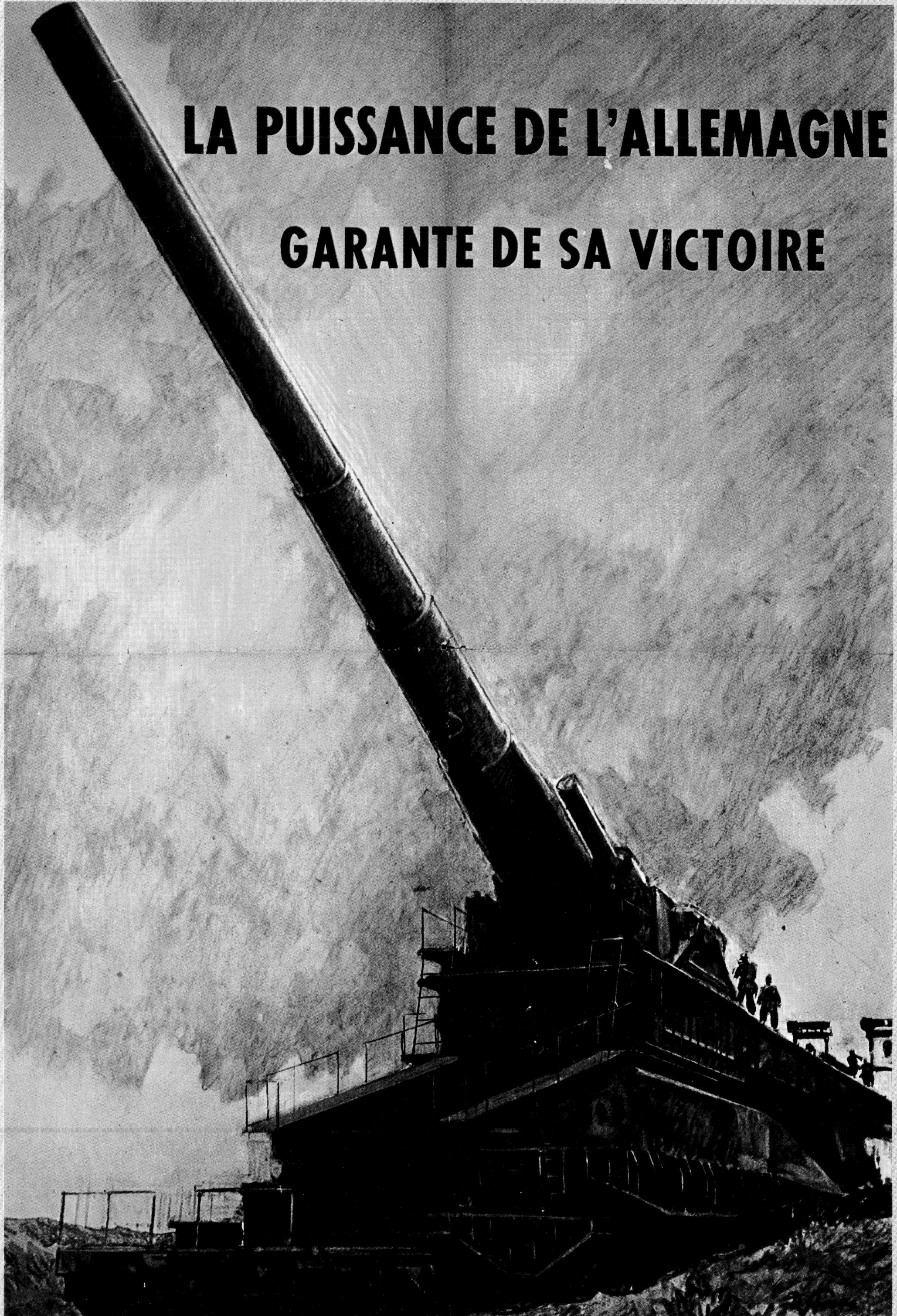

LA PUISSANCE DE L'ALLEMAGNE

GARANTE DE SA VICTOIRE

POPULATIONS
abandonnées,

faites confiance
AU SOLDAT ALLEMAND!

Left: We will win!—A pre-1943 Italian poster celebrating the combined might of the Axis powers with the flags of Italy, Japan and Germany prominently to the forefront. The countries represented in the second row are, from left to right, Rumania, Croatia, Finland, Hungary, the puppet 'Slovak State' and Bulgaria.

Below: A Free French poster, showing the swastika being crushed between the Allied hammer and the French anvil.

ENTRE LE MARTEAU ...

... ET L'ENCLUME !..

HELP CHINA

China is helping us!

PLEASE GIVE ALL YOU CAN ON

CHINA'S FLAG DAY

Right: A British poster for China, designed, probably by Nunn, for China's charity flag day. All the posters on these two pages were designed to illustrate and cement a variety of alliances, but the Belgian poster delivered its message to the Americans most simply and effectively.

Pages 90 and 91: Two German posters, one for the Danes and the other for the British. Though the Nazi view of the world was an intensely nationalist one, their concept of pure Nordic race made it possible for them to recruit for the Waffen SS, the élite Nazi army, in occupied Europe. The British poster was aimed at prisoners of war, but without any effect.

FOR DANMARK!
MOD BOLCHEVISMEN!

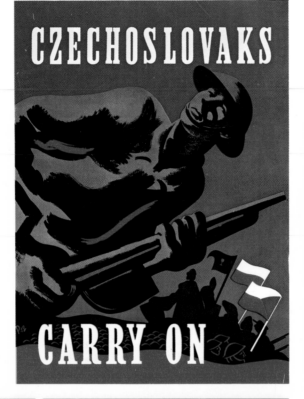

This page: Posters designed to remind Americans that the smaller peoples of occupied Europe went on fighting the Germans. The Czechoslovak and the Dutch posters were designed by the same artist, using a similar action-drawing technique; the more stylized Greek poster was designed by E. McKnight Kauffer. All three posters were designed for the American Artists for Victory competition in 1942.

Right: This charity poster in aid of Yugoslav prisoners of war makes its appeal directly, but with some subtlety in its design.

LA VICTOIRE DES NATIONS UNIES
EST MAINTENANT CERTAINE

THE UNITED NATIONS FIGHT FOR FREEDOM

Left: The massed heavy armaments and the prominently displayed flags lend support for the theory that 'The Victory of the United Nations is Today Certain'. The point is made again in 'United' (above) and in 'United We are Strong' (above right), with an increasing sophistication. 'United' was designed by Leslie Ragan for the US Office of War Information in 1943; the other artist was Hoerner. The French poster and the 'United' poster anticipated the institutionalization of United Nations. The French resistance poster (right) on the other hand used a primitive technique, a kind of patriotic tableau.

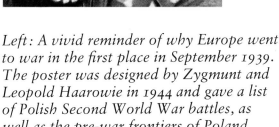

Left: A vivid reminder of why Europe went
to war in the first place in September 1939.
The poster was designed by Zygmunt and
Leopold Haarowie in 1944 and gave a list
of Polish Second World War battles, as
well as the pre-war frontiers of Poland.

Above: Italian posters celebrating the
German–Italian axis and asking for
recruits for the Italian Legion of the SS.

Right: A US poster for China, depicting an
American airman as a war-god trampling
on the Japanese aggressor.

Page 98: This poster showing a fighting
Filipino was designed for the US Office of
Special Services in March 1943, using an
intensely patriotic action painting.

Page 99: A view of the Axis (German,
Italian and Japanese) alliance, with a
shadowy samurai knight.

THE FIGHTING FILIPINOS

WE WILL ALWAYS FIGHT FOR *FREEDOM!*

Behold the Enemy
The Threat of Barbarism

The posters which concerned national security appealed to fear; the posters making various racialist, 'Red Menace' and atrocity points played on people's hatreds as well as their fear. They are the pornography of political propaganda; they have a coarse message to make.

In order to be cohesive, the nation also has, to some extent, to be exclusive; the barriers of language, habits, colour, have always tended to divide peoples into 'them' and 'us'. Xenophobia is more frequent than xenophilia; the outsider may be regarded as being unwelcome or inhuman or both. This tendency is more or less pronounced in different ethnic groups; and they have different degrees of ability to integrate and accommodate foreign elements within them. In wartime, the tendency becomes necessarily stronger; the world is visibly divided.

First World War posters used the atrocity theme frequently: the enemy was inhuman; he could not be trusted to behave decently. The charge of inhumanity was frequently made by the British against the Germans and the other way round. The Germans also started to develop a vaguer, but an equally threatening theme of the 'yellow peril' when Japan adhered to the other alliance.

It was, however, anti-Semitism which came to play a special role in Germany's propaganda in the Second World War. There was a good reason for this. Anti-Semitism was the special gift Hitler gave the Nazi movement; it became the most consistent element of Nazi ideology and propaganda. It was also the nastiest.

Opposite: In the last stages of the war— probably towards the end of 1944— Mjölnir put the alternatives before the Germans, and he put them very simply: 'Victory or Bolshevism'. The happy mother with her baby in the light part of the poster is contrasted with the sub-human, almost certainly Jewish, Bolshevik enemy in the dark half, overlooking the destruction of the German people. The poster is crudely dualistic, a kind of poster Mjölnir was not accustomed to designing.

Hitler's family came from the Waldviertel, even nowadays a remote and isolated province of Austria; its racial purity was the result of inter-marriage and the fact that those few outsiders who happened to pass through it never gave a thought to the possibility of settling there. Hitler spent several years before 1914 in Vienna, the scene of national antagonisms and, more importantly, the cradle of anti-Semitism. Well before the turn of the century, anti-Semitism became a political issue here. The Jews, the outsiders within the walls of the city, were accused of being the quintessential city-dwellers. (For centuries, they could not own land in many parts of Christian Europe). They had mastered the ways of the city: the complexities of modern finance, laws, industry and trade. At the same time, in the second half of the nineteenth century, the people from the countryside began arriving, and building, in the industrial suburbs of the old city. The simple country ways were thereby broken up; the battle-lines were laid down between the city centre and its industrial suburbs. Many of the residents of the Vienna suburbs became an easy prey for anti-Semitic ideas; it was in Vienna that policitians first started making large political capital out of anti-Semitism. Young Hitler took good note of this, and the Jews became first the scapegoats and then the victims of the Nazi movement. Such was the source and inspiration of a vast number of Nazi anti-Semitic posters before the war; the theme was used frequently during the war as well.

In particular, Nazi anti-Semitic lunacy was spread to the occupied countries. In Vichy France, it was argued in poster form that the Jews had inspired the Allied 'theft' of French North Africa; that 98% of American bankers were Jewish; that 97% of the US press was owned by the Jews. The Flemish population of Belgium was asked to fight the English

Below: A poster inviting the Flemings to join their Langemarck SS *division in April 1944. It combined recruitment with anti-Semitism; the Jew was, in this case, British.*

Above: Ninety-seven per cent of the US press was controlled by the Jews, this Vichy French poster claimed. The poster was based on the spurious findings of sociology, to which Nazi propagandists were partial. This is, however, one of the few examples of Nazi sociology translated into poster terms.

Right: The Jew, this time the Bolshevik Jew. The anti-Semitic and anti-Soviet propaganda lines merged into one so frequently that they are sometimes impossible to tell apart. Bolshevism threatened the Germans if they lost the war; therefore, in the words of the poster, they had to 'Fight until Victory'.

Jewry in the *Waffen* SS; the whole war was presented as a Jewish conspiracy against Europe.

There are other examples of racialist posters, though they are a minor vein in wartime propaganda. One of the US 'This is the Enemy' posters sets off the Japanese yellow peril against the background of a white female body, murder and arson; one of the last Italian fascist posters to be made showed the desecration of a place of worship by a black Allied soldier. However, German propaganda as well as posters contained, apart from anti-Semitism, another racial theme: the subhuman nature of the Slavs, and the Russians in particular. Anti-Semitic and *Untermensch* posters portrayed the Jews and the Slavs as being inhuman; they therefore aided, abetted and encouraged inhumanity against them.

There was a point where these two themes—anti-Semitism and the *Untermensch* propaganda—coalesced with yet another theme. This was the 'Red Menace' propaganda. The 'Jewish Conspiracy against Europe!' poster linked the subhuman Slav with the wily Jew; the menace was implied in the poster. Occasionally, the 'Red Menace' theme was used on its own, especially when it was linked with the theme of united Europe.

But the Nazi anti-Bolshevik campaign could not maintain even a small amount of detachment. The Communists at home and abroad—with the exception of the brief respite during the Molotov-Ribbentrop

pact—had long been the Nazi's main adversaries; in fact, they had joined the Jews as Enemies of the People Number 2 (this did not matter as, for the Nazis, most Bolsheviks were Jews) long before the war. This was probably the reason why the anti-Communist poster propaganda so easily fitted into the atrocity mould. The 'Die Gefahr des Bolshewismus'—'The Danger of Bolshevism'—poster is an excellent example of this important school; it uses a few colours and a lot of negative symbols: death, blood, graves, gallows, fire. In that respect it is so overloaded that it almost fails to make its point.

Atrocity and religious themes, we have already seen, were more frequently encountered in the First than in the Second World War. Nevertheless, one of the atrocity posters—it is a comment rather than hard-sell propaganda—makes skilful use of the quotation by Hitler, 'One is either a German or a Christian . . . you cannot be both', turning it against him with a vengeance. That poster is an example of 'soft' atrocity propaganda; and so is, in a way, the indignant US poster on the theme 'Remember Dec. 7th!'. But propaganda of atrocity is usually made up of harsher elements—as in the anti-British Dunkerque poster, for instance.

Opposite: The Jewish plot against Europe finally revealed. Since the forgery of the Protocols of the Elders of Zion *early in the twentieth century, the global Jewish conspiracy had been a favourite theme of European anti-Semites. The steel-plated 'Fortress Europe' of the poster could, without doubt, resist the unholy Jewish alliance; at least the British Jew has not got blood-stained fingers.*

Left: A German poster for the Ukraine. This is a straight 'atrocities' poster, describing Stalin as a bloodthirsty, arson-loving tyrant who was about to lose the war. Inserted on the left is the 'Programme of blood-thirsty Stalin'; the poster is a good example of atrocity propaganda which wastes no subtlety in making its point.

Page 106: This German 'Bolshevik Danger' poster is overloaded with symbols of atrocity—the sinister, cloaked figure; the dagger dripping blood, the gallows, cemetery and conflagration in the background. This kitsch poster is so awful in its conception and execution that it is in a class of its own in atrocity propaganda.

Page 107: The ghostly figures against the cold, wintry background of 'Europe United against Bolshevism' do not help to establish the point the poster is trying to make. The German-inspired poster for occupied France failed mainly because of the anonymity and other-worldly quality of its figures.

L'EUROPE UNIE

CONTRE LE BOLCHEVISME

"ONE IS EITHER A GERMAN
OR A CHRISTIAN . . . . .
YOU CANNOT BE BOTH."
—ADOLF HITLER, 1933.

14

*Left: An example of British atrocity
propaganda. It at least tries to make a valid
point by juxtaposing the text, a quote from
a speech by Hitler, with the photograph of
a bombed-out town. An unusually
thoughtful poster, for its kind.*

*Right and below right: Two US posters
explaining the nature of the enemy. The
female form, and 'soft' pornography, were
frequently employed in the horror posters
of the Second World War. There is little to
choose between the Japanese rapist and the
killer in the background, Hitler.*

*Page 110: A Vichy poster illustrating the
evacuation of Dunkerque in 1940 for the
benefit of defeated Frenchmen. Those who
did not get a place on British ships during
the evacuation did not, the poster implies,
miss very much.*

*Page 111: A less effective poster produced
by the Vichy French. It turns back to the
development of Anglo-French colonial
rivalries. It makes an historical point
clumsily, and uses far too much text to
explain its message. The only interesting
technical feature of the poster is the use of
the British bulldog as a negative symbol.*

1940. DUNKERQUE. LES ANGLAIS S'OPPOSENT A
L'EMBARQUEMENT DES DERNIERS FRANÇAIS
QUI VENAIENT DE PROTÉGER LEUR RETRAITE

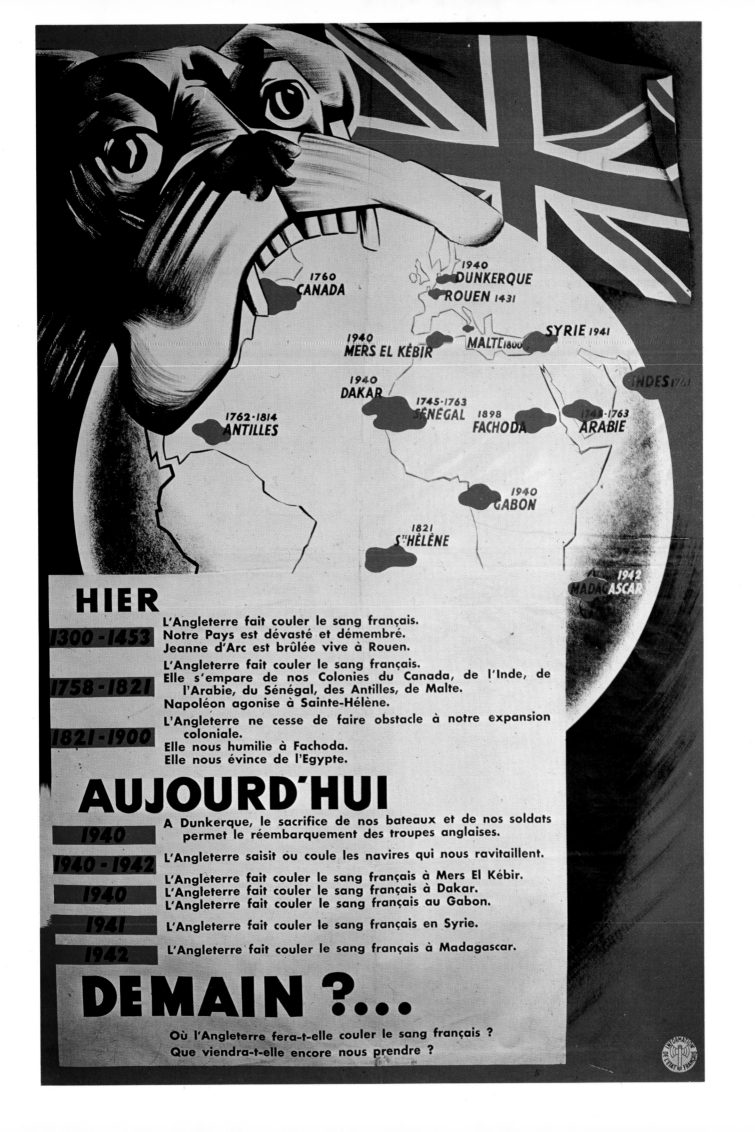

Left and right: Two US posters attempting to explain the bestiality, or at least the unreasonableness in the case of the second poster, of the Japanese. The patriotic symbol is so tattered in the poster commemorating the Japanese attack on Pearl Harbor, and the background so violent, that the message of the poster amounts to a message of atrocity. The use of Admiral Yamamoto's head is also intended to repel the viewer and set off a racialist or at least xenophobic reaction in him.

Pages 114 and 115: Italian posters on the subject of the enemy's inhumanity. Nazi propaganda had been using the theme of US 'gangster pilots' for some time; air raids aimed at the civilian population were an expression of their 'gangster' character. The second poster adds a racial motif to its theme. The destruction of European Christian civilization by alien troops is the poster's main message.

"I am looking forward to dictating peace to the United States in the White House at Washington"
— ADMIRAL YAMAMOTO

What do YOU say, AMERICA?

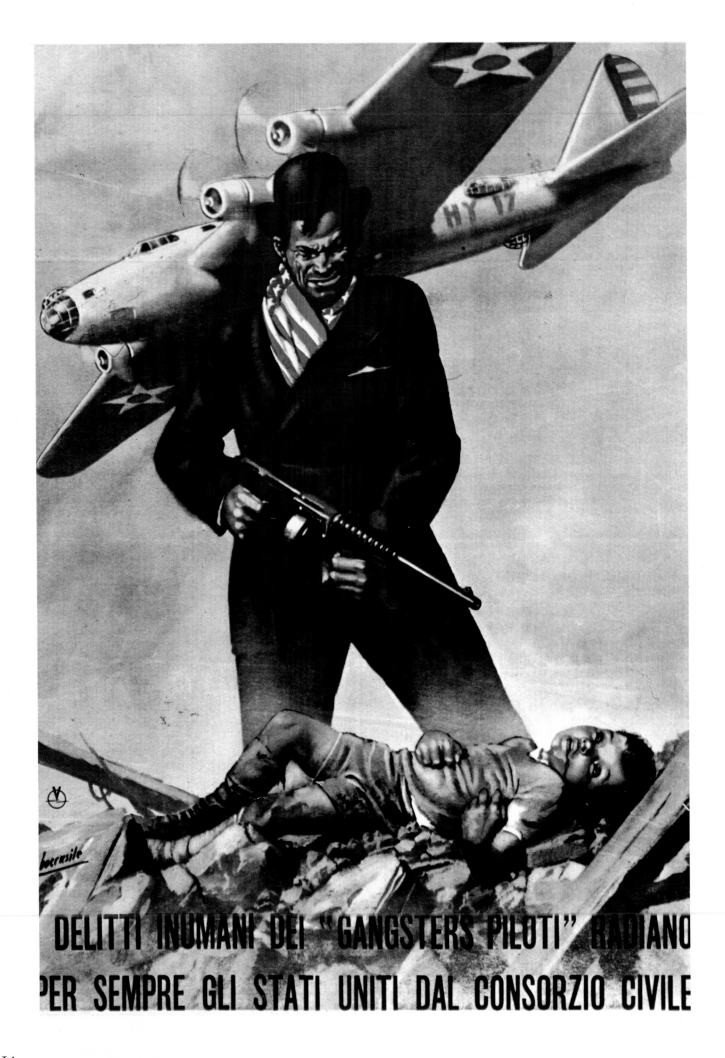

*Left: The Italian version of a famous
American poster by Karl Kochler and
Victor Ancona. It is perhaps the most
sophisticated example of atrocity
propaganda to have emerged out of the
war. The poster won the first prize in the
'Nature of the Enemy' part in the US
Artists for Victory competition in 1942.
This was probably the best organized
competition out of a number of similar
events in America during the war. Over
2,200 entries were received, and the
prize-winning posters were shown at the
New York Museum of Modern Art.*

*Right: S. Lipinski's poster, printed in
Rome after the liberation of the capital by
Allied troops. It commemorates the
destruction of Warsaw after the outbreak
of the war and then in the Warsaw
uprising of 1944. It made its point in a
comparatively mild way, underscoring it
with a restrained use of a religious symbol.*

*Page 118: The well-known Soviet poster
'Revenge', by Shmaridov, published in
November 1942. It uses the mother-and-
child symbol to illustrate the horrors of
war; artists in all the belligerent countries
used similar themes. It is atrocity
propaganda, but it uses strong, positive
symbols.*

*Page 119: R. S. R. Candappa's poster
illustrates the Japanese squeeze on other
Asian peoples, for the sake of so-called
'Japanese co-prosperity'. It was printed in
1943, and was unusual in that it used the
vehicle and technique of atrocity
propaganda to make an economic point.*

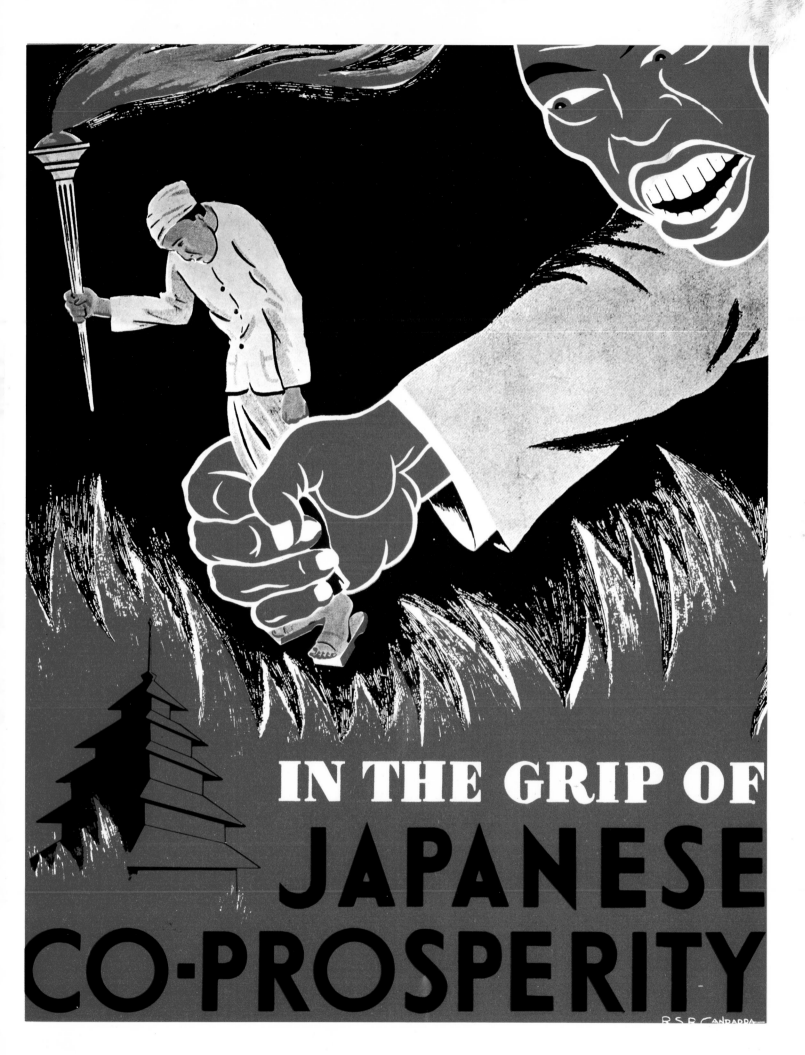

IN THE GRIP OF
JAPANESE
CO-PROSPERITY

Index

References to illustrations in italics

Ancona, Victor *116*
Anti-Semitism 14, *14*, 15, *15*, 22, 23, 101–3, *101–4*, 105
Artists for Victory competition 50, 92, 116
Asquith, Lord 10
Atelier Albrecht *75*
Atherton, John *50*

Bairnsfather, Bruce 32, *59*
Bairnsfather, Thomas 32
Barclay, McClelland 42
Beaverbrook, Lord 10
Bird, Cyril Kenneth *59*
Bocasili, Gino *53*
Bormann, Martin 24
British Broadcasting Corporation 17, 20, 24, 25, 82
Broadcasting as propaganda weapon 11, 15, 19, 20–1, 25, 26
Buehler, Philipp 13

Candappa, R.S.R. *119*
Carlu, Jean *69*
Carr, Leslie *68*
Churchill, Winston 22, 24, 34, 37, 88
Colin, Paul *61*

Dali, Salvador *50*
Department for Enemy Propaganda (British) 17
Dohanos, Stevan *48*

Films as propaganda weapon 11, 15, 20, 26–7

First World War, propaganda during 8, 9, *11*, 9–12, 13, 26, 27, 28, 32, 59, 101
Fougasse *see* Bird, Cyril Kenneth
Franco, Francisco 8

Games, Abram 57, *59*, *60*
Goebbels, Joseph Paul 14, 15, *16*, 17, 18–21, 22, 23, 24, 25, 26, 37
Gregory XV, Pope 12, 13
Guignon, Henri *34*, *37*

Haarowie, Leopold and Zygmunt *96*
Halifax, Lord 82
Hansi *43*, *44*
Hitler, Adolf 7–8, 12–15, 17, 18, 20, 21, 49, 64, *108*; attitude to propaganda 12–13; Goebbels's presentation of him 15; portrayed in enemy posters *19*, *20*, *21*, *67*, *109*; portrayed in Nazi posters *17*, *39*
Hoerner *95*

Kauffer, E. McKnight *92*
Kitchener, Lord *11*
Kochler, Karl *116*

Leaflets as propaganda weapon 11, 20, 26, 27, 27–8, 29
Lenin, Nikolai (Vladimir Ilyich Ulyanov) 8, 12, 15
Lipinski, S. *117*
Lloyd George, David 10
Lockhart, Sir Robert Bruce 18
Lusitania 11

Martin, David Stone *70*
Masterman, Charles 10, 26
Mein Kampf 12, 13
Monroe, Captain James 27
Mjölnir *see* Schweitzer, Hans
Ministry of Information (British) 17, 20
Morris, G.R. *4*
Mussolini, Benito 8, 15, 21, 35

Neurath, Konstantin von 19
Northcliffe, Lord 11
Nunn 89

Petzold, W. *77*
Political Intelligence Department (British F.O.) 17, 20, 59
Political Warfare Executive (British) 18, 20
Pornography 29, 101, *109*
Posters: Axis *99*; Belgian *65*, *88*; British *4*, *36*, *57*, *59*, *60*, *66*, *67*, *68*, *83*, *89*, *108*, *112*, *113*; Finnish *55*; First World War *9*, *11*; French *33*, *43*, *44*, *61*, *62*, *64*, Free French *89*, French Resistance *95*, Vichy Government *103*, *105*, *111*; Italian *35*, *53*, *75*, *97*, *114*, *115*; Nazi *14*, *15*, *16*, *17*, 22, 23, 24, 25, *30*, *37*, *38*, *39*, *45*, *46*, *54*, *75*, *76*, *77*, *82*, *84*, *85*, *86*, *87*, *90*, *91*, *100*, *102*, *103*, *104*, *105*, *110*; Polish *6*, *96*, *117*; Soviet *16*, *18*, *19*, *20*, *21*, *40*, *41*, *47*, *78*, *79*, *80*, *118*; US *frontispiece*, *34*, *42*, *48*, *50*, *51*, *52*, *56*, *58*, *59*, *69*, *70*, *71*, *72*, *73*, *74*, *88*, *92*, *93*, *95*, *97*, *98*, *109*, *116*, *119*

Promi (Nazi Ministry of Propaganda) 19, 20, 21, 23, 25
Psychological Warfare Division (SHAEF) 18
Pym, Harold *66*

Ragan, Leslie *95*
Ribbentrop, Joachim von 19, 103
Riefenstahl, Leni 26
Roger, Yvonne *64*
Roosevelt, Franklin *66*, 74
Rothermere, Lord 11
Rotter, V. *88*

Schweitzer, Hans (Mjölnir) *30*, *37*, 37, *39*, *45*, *46*, *100*
Shmaridov *118*
SS, recruitment for *84*, *90*, *91*, *102*
Stalin, Joseph 15, 49, *80*, 105
Stoops, Herbert Morton *50*

Thomas, Bert 32
Toidze, Irakly *40*
Toussaint *33*
Triumph of the Will 27

Untermensch propaganda 22, 28, *100*, *103*, 103
US Office of Special Services 98
US Office of War Information 18, 48, 70, 95
US Treasury Department 65, 72–3

Yamamoto, Admiral Gombei *113*
Yegley *51*

Zik *30*

Bibliography

BARGHOORN, F.C. *Soviet Foreign Propaganda* (Princeton University Press, 1964)

BRAMSTED, E.K. *Goebbels and National Socialist Propaganda 1925–1945* (University of Michigan Press, 1965)

DARRACOTT, J. and LOFTUS, B. *Second World War Posters* (Imperial War Museum, London, 1972)

HALE, O.J. *The Captive Press in the Third Reich* (Princeton University Press, 1964)

HOLT, R. and van de VELDE, R. *Strategic Psychological Operations and American Policy* (University of Chicago Press, 1960)

KIRKPATRICK, I. *Mussolini: A Study in Power* (Odham's, London, 1964)

RHODES, A. *Propaganda* (Angus & Robertson, London, 1975)

QUALTER, T.H. *Propaganda and Psychological Warfare* (Random House, New York, 1962)

ZEMAN, Z.A.B. *Nazi Propaganda* (Oxford University Press, 1971)